ENGLISCH IM BERUF

English for the Energy Industry

Simon Campbell

SHORT COURSE
SERIES

Verfasser	Simon Campbell, Essen
Kritische Durchsicht	Susan Holder, Berlin Laura Scott, Düsseldorf Christiane Maria Loosen, Düsseldorf
Verlagsredaktion	Janan Barksdale, Sylee Gore
Außenredaktion	John Stevens
Redaktionelle Mitarbeit	Oliver Busch (Wortliste), Rebecca Syme
Bildredaktion	Uta Hübner
Gesamtgestaltung und technische Umsetzung	Sylvia Lang

Quellen

Titelfoto: Fontshop
Cartoons: Oxford Designers & Illustrators
Illustrationen und Symbole: Andreas Terglane, z.T. nach Vorlagen von Energywatch (S. 21), RWE Power AG (S. 32), STEAG (S. 44, 48), Vattenfall, Schweden (S. 17/Geschäftsbericht 2005, S. 24)
Fotos: Bananastock: S. 43; Corbis GmbH: S. 35; Corel: S. 5, 15, 22, 30, 36, 38, 51, 55; Comstock: S. 20; Fontshop: S. 5, 9, 14, 20, 22, 30, 33, 39, 46; Getty Images: S. 24, 26, 39; Vattenfall Europe Berlin AG & Co. KG: S. 11; F1ONLINE: S. 10/Kraus, S. 15/Pixtal; S. 50/Stuart Pearce-AGE; Getty Images: S. 41/Shiva Twin; Picture-Alliance: S. 10/akg-images, S. 25/dpa, S. 31/ZB, S. 34/dpa
Texte: Energywatch: S. 21

www.cornelsen.de

Die Webseiten Dritter, deren Internetadressen in diesem Lehrwerk angegeben sind, wurden vor Drucklegung sorgfältig geprüft. Der Verlag übernimmt keine Gewähr für die Aktualität und den Inhalt dieser Seiten oder solcher, die mit ihnen verlinkt sind.

1. Auflage, 3. Druck 2020

Alle Drucke dieser Auflage sind inhaltlich unverändert und können im Unterricht nebeneinander verwendet werden.

© 2008 Cornelsen Verlag, Berlin
© 2020 Cornelsen Verlag GmbH, Berlin

Druck: Athesiadruck GmbH

ISBN 978-3-464-20385-9

PEFC zertifiziert
Dieses Produkt stammt aus nachhaltig bewirtschafteten Wäldern und kontrollierten Quellen.
www.pefc.de

PEFC/18-31-166

Contents

PAGE	UNIT	TOPICS	USEFUL LANGUAGE AND SKILLS
5	**1 Introduction to the energy business**	Fuels and energy sources Types of power plant Supplying the customer Profile of an energy company Regulation of the energy market The future of the gas market	Telephoning for information Expressing opinions and (dis)agreement
14	**2 Markets and customers**	Residential, business and industrial customers Supplying an industrial customer Breakdown in supply Customer choice Consumer watchdogs	Describing trends, developments and consequences Replying to letters of complaint Dealing with a complaint
22	**3 Emissions and the environment**	Energy saving The image of the energy industry Technical measures to reduce pollution The cost of protecting the environment Emissions trading The Kyoto Protocol	Replying to invitations Giving a presentation
30	**4 The nuclear issue**	Developments in nuclear power The nuclear production process Safety and security issues Reprocessing and waste disposal Arguments for and against nuclear power Nuclear fusion	Describing a process Chairing a meeting
39	**5 Investment plans**	Mergers and takeovers SWOT analyses Financial documents Assets, equity and liabilities Coal power plants Disinvestment	Discussion in a meeting
46	**6 The future of energy**	Future production, demand and supply Departments and their functions The fuel cell The hydrogen economy Lack of vision in the energy industry	Writing reports

PAGE	APPENDIX
54	**Test yourself!**
56	**Partner files**
59	**Answer key**
64	**Transcripts**
69	**A–Z word list**
76	**Glossary**
78	**Useful phrases and vocabulary**
80	**Abbreviations, acronyms and numbers**

Vorwort

English for the Energy Industry bietet Beschäftigten in Energieunternehmen und verwandten Sparten sowie allen interessierten Lernenden notwendige sprachliche Mittel, um über die komplexen Strukturen und Entwicklungen auf dem globalen Energiemarkt kommunizieren und typische Situationen des Berufsalltags in diesen Bereichen bewältigen zu können.

English for the Energy Industry ist in sechs Units unterteilt. Jede Unit hat einen eigenen thematischen Schwerpunkt. So behandelt der Kurs Themen, die für Beschäftigte in verschiedenen Positionen und Funktionen relevant sind: Energieerzeugung und -verteilung, Umwelttechnik, Vertrieb und Verkauf, PR, Unternehmenspolitik und -strategie. Die Units können je nach Interesse und Bedarf in beliebiger Reihenfolge und damit unabhängig voneinander bearbeitet werden. Es empfiehlt sich allerdings, mit Unit 1 zu beginnen, da diese einen Überblick über die verschiedenen Bereiche bietet.

Alle Units sind logisch und systematisch aufgebaut, sodass bestmögliche Lernresultate erzielt werden können. **Switch On** leitet jede Unit ein und bereitet auf die thematischen Inhalte der Lerneinheit vor. Neue Sprach- und Redemittel werden zunächst in Hörverständnisübungen (mit Audio-CD) präsentiert, die eine Reihe von authentischen Situationen aus der Energiewirtschaft aufgreifen. Mithilfe der nachfolgenden freien Übungen werden dann die neu erworbenen Redemittel eingeübt und angewandt. Dieser Prozess wird von Bildmaterial und hilfreichen Illustrationen unterstützt.

Realitätsnahe Rollenspiele – mit Rollenkarten in den **Partner Files** im Anhang – schaffen konkrete Sprechanlässe zu energiebezogenen Themen. Situationen aus dem Arbeitsalltag werden aufgegriffen und nachgestellt, um so wichtige Sprachmittel praxisbezogen einzusetzen.
Auch werden in jeder Unit systematisch eine Reihe von **useful phrases** erarbeitet, die nicht zuletzt in den Partnerübungen Anwendung finden.

Eines der Hauptziele von **English for the Energy Industry** besteht darin, Lernenden den zur Erreichung ihrer kommunikativen Ziele nötigen Wortschatz – einschließlich fachspezifischer Terminologie – zu vermitteln. Jede Unit stellt andere, der jeweiligen Thematik entsprechende Wortfelder dar. Zu vielen Aufgaben gibt es einen **Vocabulary Assistant**, der wichtige Wörter und Redewendungen auflistet und so das Verständnis unmittelbar erleichtert.

In **Switch Off** am Ende einer jeden Unit findet sich ein Text, der gedanklich die Thematik der Unit weiterführt und auch sprachlich anspruchsvoll ist. Diese Texte behandeln geschäftliche, technische und politische Aspekte und fordern zu persönlicher Stellungnahme und Diskussion auf.

Nach erfolgreichem Abschluss aller Units können Sie mithilfe eines Kreuzworträtsels in **Test Yourself** wichtiges Vokabular aus dem **Short Course** in komprimierter Form wiederholen.

Im Anhang von **English for the Energy Industry** finden Sie einen **Answer key**, mit dem Sie Ihre Lösungen selbstständig überprüfen können. Dieser Lösungsschlüssel ist besonders für die Lernenden hilfreich, die dieses Buch im Selbststudium bearbeiten. Der Anhang enthält ferner die **Partner files** sowie eine zweisprachige **A–Z word list**. Darüber hinaus finden sich hier nützliche Übersichten und Auflistungen zu den Themen des Buches. Besonders Letztere erlauben Ihnen, auch am Arbeitsplatz die gebräuchlichsten Fachbegriffe, Redewendungen, Abkürzungen und Maßeinheiten schnell und sicher nachzuschlagen.

Introduction to the energy business

Switch on

Work with a partner. Sort the fuels and energy sources below into the correct category. Can you add any more to the lists?

fossil fuel(s)	renewables	nuclear fuel(s)

(hard) coal   wind   oil   sun

uranium   gas   biomass   lignite

Now answer these questions.

1 What fuels and sources are used at your company, or the companies you do business with?
2 Which one is used most?
3 Where do these fuels come from?
4 Which are imported?

1 Match these different power plants to their descriptions.

1 hydro power plant
2 solar power plant
3 nuclear power plant
4 wind power plant
5 gas-fired power plant
6 run-of-river power plant
7 coal-fired power plant
8 lignite-fired power plant
9 pump-storage power plant

a a traditional type of power plant which burns a solid, black fossil fuel
b a power plant which pumps water back uphill into a reservoir during periods of low demand
c a plant which uses the flow of water from a reservoir to generate electricity
d a power station utilizing the natural flow of water in a river for generating power
e a controversial type of power plant that uses uranium as its primary fuel
f a power plant which uses the natural flow of air to generate electricity
g a fossil fuel power plant which burns a solid, dark brown fuel
h a power plant that generates electricity utilizing energy from the sun
i a power station which burns gas as its primary fuel

2

2 **Listen to a phone call between a journalist, Colin Maitland, and the public relations officer of the company ELEC, Maria Berger. Complete the journalist's notes.**

> <u>ELEC'S fossil fuel use</u>
> _____ 1 and _____ 2
>
> <u>Power plants and loads</u>
> Lignite-fired plants for _____ 3 load
> Gas-fired plants for _____ 4 and peak-load ranges
> Gas plants also used to supply _____ 5
>
> <u>Technology to protect environment</u>
> ELEC say they have _____ 6 equipment installed in their plants.
>
> <u>Altrath plant, near Berlin</u>
> Commissioned in _____ 7 but has been _____ 8
> since then.
>
> <u>Wind generation</u>
> Company building more power stations, but difficult to get _____
> _____ 9 in some countries. ELEC views criticism that these
> _____ 10 the countryside as 'exaggerated'.

What other questions would you expect the journalist to ask?

<table>
<tr><td rowspan="5">**VOCABULARY ASSISTANT**</td><td>base load *Grundlast*   to commission *in Betrieb nehmen*</td></tr>
<tr><td>district heating *Fernwärme*   installed capacity *installierte Leistung*</td></tr>
<tr><td>intermediate/medium load *Mittellast*   peak load *Spitzenlast*</td></tr>
<tr><td>to retrofit *nachrüsten*</td></tr>
</table>

3 **Make phrases from the dialogue by matching a word on the left to one on the right. Listen to the dialogue again to check your answers.**

1	base	a	equipment
2	company	b	fuels
3	electricity	c	heating
4	energy	d	mix
5	fossil	e	policy
6	power	f	production
7	district	g	station
8	state-of-the-art	h	load

Match the expressions you have just formed to the following definitions.

9 _____ _____ = the generation of electrical power

10 _____ _____ = energy sources such as gas, oil and coal, but not water and wind

11 _____ _____ = the power level at which basic demand and consumption is covered

12 _____ _____ = apparatus of the latest technological level

13 _____ _____ = the different primary fuels and sources used for energy production

14 _____ _____ = a plan of action chosen by a business or firm

15 _____ _____ = a plant in which electricity is produced

16 _____ _____ = a system of distributing heat in one centralized location, often linked to a power plant

4 Work with a partner to do this role-play.

The journalist Colin Maitland needs further information about ELEC's power plants, but the public relations officer is away. You and a colleague must put the information together. Use phrases from the box below.

PARTNER FILES Partner A File 1, p. 56
Partner B File 7, p. 57

TELEPHONING FOR INFORMATION

Introductions
Hello … . This is … speaking.
Good morning. Is that …?
Hi …, it's … here.

Asking for information
I need some information about …
I'd like to have some (more) information about …
Can/Could you give me more information about …?
Can/Could you please tell me (about) …?
Who / What / When / Where / Why / How …?
What about …?

Asking for repetition
Sorry, I didn't quite catch that.
Would you mind repeating that?

Positive response
Sure.
No problem.
I'd be happy to.

Negative response
I'm afraid I can't help you there.
I'm afraid not.

DID YOU KNOW?

In Anglo-Saxon cultures being polite is very important; this also applies to communication in business. For example, the phrase 'I was wondering …' can be used for requests, as in 'I was wondering if you could send the information again.' Phrases such as 'I'm afraid', 'Well actually' and 'unfortunately' are used to introduce something negative or make complaints. Look at these examples:
  'May I smoke?' – 'Well actually, it is forbidden in this building.'
  'I'm afraid the last bill was not accurate.'
Not using such phrases can be seen as being too direct.

5 **Read what people say about different fuels and energy sources. Which bubble is mainly about the following?**

1 public perception of energy and the energy industry
2 the effects on the environment of different sources of energy
3 the availability of renewable sources
4 the reliability and efficiency of fossil fuels

a
Coal and lignite are the most reliable fuels. We'll depend on them more as gas and oil disappear. There may be a few problems with emissions, but these can easily be solved. They're also very versatile and can be used to produce electricity and heat our homes efficiently.

b
Fossil fuels are harmful; think how they affect our atmosphere and countryside. We can't build our future energy planning on them. We have to think differently. The sun is a clean energy source, and the potential for providing us with power is enormous! What's more we can install solar cells on buildings, which will reduce the requirement for large power stations.

c
Solar power is good as far as it goes, but what do you do when the sun isn't shining? In northern Europe there are often cloudy skies, and in some countries there are only four hours of sunlight per day in winter. Wind on the other hand is always at our disposal – more than the sun anyway. We can use this source to cover our needs.

d
The most important thing is to educate people about energy. It may be true that fossil fuels and other sources have some drawbacks, but there are many positive aspects. We should focus on informing people; how they see energy is important.

Say which statements you agree with. Use phrases from below.

EXPRESSING OPINIONS AND (DIS)AGREEMENT

Giving your opinion
I think/feel (that) …
In my opinion …
In my view …

Clarifying
So you're saying …
You mean …
What do you mean exactly by …?

Agreeing
Quite right.
That's true.
I quite agree.

Disagreeing
Yes, but …
Actually, I think …
To be honest …
I don't quite agree.

Asking for opinions
What do you think?
How do you see it?

6 **Work with a partner. How do you rate these different types of power plant on a scale from 1 (= good) to 6 (= very poor/bad)? Use the phrases on page 8.**

Power Plant Type	Rating				
	Public perception	Effects on environment	Availability of primary fuel/source	Reliability	Efficiency
Hydro power plant					
Solar power plant					
Nuclear power plant					
Wind power plant					
Gas-fired power plant					
Lignite-fired power plant					
Biomass-fired power plant					

Compare your results with other students and give reasons for your rating.

7 **ELEC is creating some basic educational publicity material. Complete these statements with the missing expressions, and then number the statements in the correct order.**

connection • distribution network • facility • municipal utility •
overhead lines • supplier • transmission network

a   And that is how the power eventually reaches you, via the _____ that links your home to the network.

1   b   From the power station, high-voltage electricity enters what we call the _____.

c   The utility transmits, distributes and delivers electricity (and possibly gas) from a _____ which it owns and operates to the final customer. Delivery is via what we call the _____.

d   This supplier is the company from whom you, the customer, get your energy. It is often a _____, owned by a city or town.

e   This is a system of transmission towers and _____, through which the electricity makes its way to the _____.

8 **Complete this text from ELEC's website with the correct verb forms.**

The Players
of the **Power Business**

| About ELEC → | Energy supply → | How it works → | | Keyword search 🔍 |

From generator to supplier to customer

Electricity _is generated_ [1] (generate) by power stations and _____ [2] (feed) into the high-voltage transmission network. Via transmission towers and overhead lines it _____ [3] (transport) to the local supplier, an organization which _____ [4] (own) by the municipality or the regional subsidiary of a larger power company. This local supplier is normally the first point of contact for the customer. Connections _____ [5] (organize) by this company, and power _____ [6] (deliver) to the customer.

Customer choice and the role of the regulator

In some countries the supplier can _____ [7] (choose) by the customer as some markets _____ [8] (liberalize). In order to ensure that there is fair competition some states have set up regulators. Their main task is to ensure that there is non-discriminatory third-party access. The grid fees that the operators charge for using the networks _____ [9] (also control). When prices _____ [10] (increase) by the supplier, this _____ [11] (also monitor) by the regulator.

ⓘ Site map   ⓘ Legal   ⓘ Access   ⓘ Disclaimer

VOCABULARY ASSISTANT

grid fee _Netznutzungsentgelt_   high voltage _Hochspannung_
municipality _Kommune_   subsidiary _Tochtergesellschaft_
third-party access _Durchleitung_

DID YOU KNOW?

The first practical generator was built by Thomas Edison, the famous inventor. He used it to provide electricity for his laboratory and then later to generate power for the first New York street to be illuminated by electric lamps. Unlike most AC (alternating current) generators of today, Edison's apparatus produced DC (direct current).

9 **Find a word or expression in the text in exercise 8 which means the same as the following.**

1 pylon
2 a company owned by a parent company
3 country
4 to watch and check continuously

5 to make certain
6 grid
7 to demand an amount of money for goods or services

10 **Complete this table and then the text below with the right word or expression.**

	Noun	Verb	Company/Person
1	generation		generator
2	transmission		
3	sales		
4		to distribute	
5		to regulate	
6		to liberalize	– – –
7	supply		

Is the regulator the answer?

In European countries where the energy market has been liberalized, many energy customers are not pleased with the results of this _____[8] process. They claim there are no real benefits. They see energy companies making large profits firstly through the _____[9] of power and then as grid operators when they charge outside companies high grid fees for the _____[10] of electricity through their networks. Many see _____[11] as the answer as this should force companies to consider their prices. This will probably make it less profitable to _____[12] the final customer with electricity and gas. Each company´s overall _____[13] volume is set to decrease as more firms enter the market.

> **DID YOU KNOW?**
>
> In some countries the company which operates a high-voltage grid is called the TSO (Transmission Systems Operator). The company which runs a distribution network is sometimes called the DSO (Distribution Systems Operator).

11 At a follow-up meeting to the phone call in exercise 2, Maria explains ELEC's structure to Colin. Listen to her explanation and complete this chart taken from ELEC's annual report. Then say which division the statements under the chart refer to.

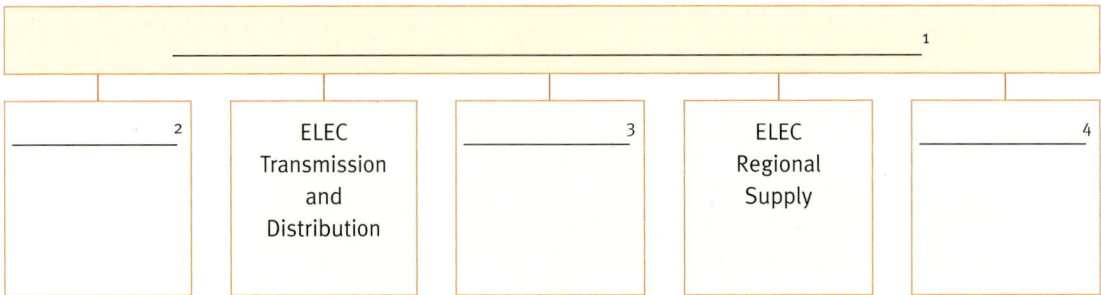

| _____ 2 | ELEC Transmission and Distribution | _____ 3 | ELEC Regional Supply | _____ 4 |

5   It has networks in many European countries.
6   It is a buying operation, procuring energy for the European supply company.
7   It procures gas from partners in Russia.
8   It is a company in its own right.
9   It runs opencast mines producing lignite and coal.
10 This division has a lot of subsidiaries each responsible for a specific geographical area.
11 This division is in the process of being consolidated under one management structure.

Now outline the structure of the company you work for or do business with. How does it compare to ELEC´s structure?

VOCABULARY ASSISTANT
customer proximity   *Kundennähe*
opencast mines   *Tagebau*
to procure   *beschaffen*

12 Complete this puzzle and find the person who buys electricity or gas. The answers are all words from this unit. Who is the person in column a?

1   a fossil fuel used for generating electricity
2   a company which transports electricity to homes and businesses
3   the first of the three load levels; the other two are 'intermediate' and 'peak'
4   a company that generates, transmits, distributes and supplies electricity or gas from facilities which it owns and operates
5   a company which runs a network system
6   the process whereby a company transports electricity at high-voltage levels
7   a company which produces electricity
8   what a company is involved in when it buys and sells electricity or gas at the energy exchanges

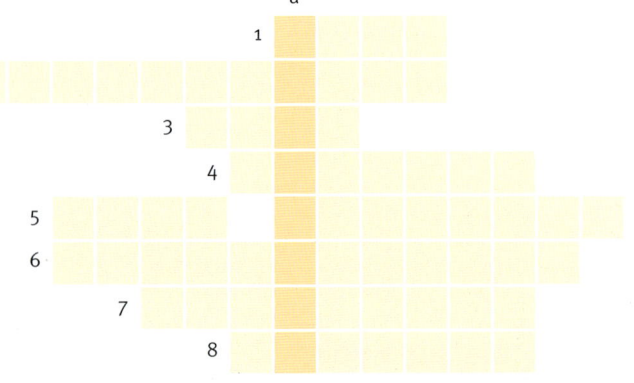

Switch off

Which countries does your country import its gas from? Read this newspaper article and discuss the questions.

Issues

Gas in Crisis?

The world is changing. There is an energy crisis on the horizon for Europe. If we take natural gas as an example it would seem at first glance that countries such as Norway, Britain and the Nether-

lands have sufficient gas reserves to supply Europe for some time to come. However, this is misleading; most of these reserves will be used up over the next 10 to 20 years. Even if more deposits are found in the North Sea or the Atlantic Ocean the problem will still not be solved. The continent must turn to Russia where there are huge quantities

of gas underground. This country is in the happy position of being the gas giant of the world.

But other nations are also approaching Moscow to cover their energy requirements. The economies of countries such as China and India are expanding dramatically and they are going to need massive amounts of energy, which includes gas. Will there be enough of this commodity to satisfy the needs of Asia and Europe? This is by no means certain, and the consequence could be a shortage of gas imports, which could lead to power cuts in some European countries in the future.

There is one other source of gas – LNG, liquefied natural gas. This is transported by ship from such places as the Arabian Peninsula. Nevertheless, it is questionable if these supplies can ever be a realistic alternative to gas which is imported by pipeline; the simple fact is that the volumes shipped would never meet demand.

People are therefore right to be worried. Political leaders and companies must tackle this issue; we need a secure and reliable supply of gas for the long term. This inevitably means that wholesale prices will soar, but this is still better than the nightmare scenario of freezing in our homes or having no power for our industry.

Over to you

- Is there really a gas crisis? What do you think?
- What about oil and coal? Do you think there will be enough reserves for the future?
- How do you think China will develop its economy and how will it power its industry?
- How can your country ensure gas supplies?

2 Markets and customers

Switch on

Discuss the questions with a partner.

- Have you ever switched your gas or electricity supplier?
- How easy is it to do? What would encourage you to do it, or prevent you from doing it?

Now decide how important the following factors would be if you wanted to switch your electricity and/or gas supplier?

The new supplier should	Very important	Not so important
1 offer a cheaper price than the current supplier.	☐	☐
2 guarantee security of supply.	☐	☐
3 supply both electricity and gas.	☐	☐
4 take care of all formalities regarding the changeover from the old to the new contract.	☐	☐
5 send clear and accurate bills.	☐	☐
6 offer the customer different ways of paying bills (direct debit, credit card, etc).	☐	☐
7 provide online services (eg for meter readings).	☐	☐
8 give advice on energy efficiency.	☐	☐
9 have a 24-hour helpline (call centre).	☐	☐
10 have offices in the same town as my home.	☐	☐

VOCABULARY ASSISTANT

direct debit *Einzugsermächtigung*
to encourage *ermutigen*
meter *Zähler*
meter reading *Zählerstand, Zählerablesung*

1 **Work with a partner. How are these types of customer defined in the company you work for? Give examples for each one.**

1 a residential/retail customer
2 a business customer
3 an industrial customer

Discuss the following questions about industrial customers.

1 What are the largest five industries in your country or region? Use those listed below to help you. What are their products? Who are their clients?
2 How are they supplied with power? Do some of them have their own power plants or are they supplied by other energy companies?
3 Which consume(s) the most energy? Rank them on a scale of 1–5 according to how much electricity they consume.
4 What do large industrial companies want from energy companies?

Industries

aluminium industry • chemical industry • steel industry • pharmaceutical industry • pulp and paper industry • plastic industry • textile industry • automotive industry

4

2 **Paul Nieuwenhuis from AECP – the Association of European Chemical Producers – is talking to Anna Schmidt from the energy company ELEC. You are sitting in on the meeting. Listen and decide whether the statements below are true or false.**

1 AECP has established an energy procurement unit.
2 Its aim is to harmonize the terms under which it does business with its various suppliers.
3 AECP wants there to be one key account manager at ELEC.
4 A key issue for AECP is security of supply.
5 AECP expects its requirements to remain constant.

Listen to the dialogue again and take notes for the minutes of the meeting. Include the following sections: 1 Members of AECP; 2 Development of wholesale prices; 3 AECP's objectives; 4 Forecasts on AECP's future energy consumption; 5 Next step.

VOCABULARY ASSISTANT

procurement *Beschaffung*
wholesale price *Großhandelspreis*
volatile *instabil*
consumption pattern *Verbrauchsentwicklung*

3 **These graphs show developments mentioned in exercise 2. What does each graph show? If you are not sure, listen to the dialogue again.**

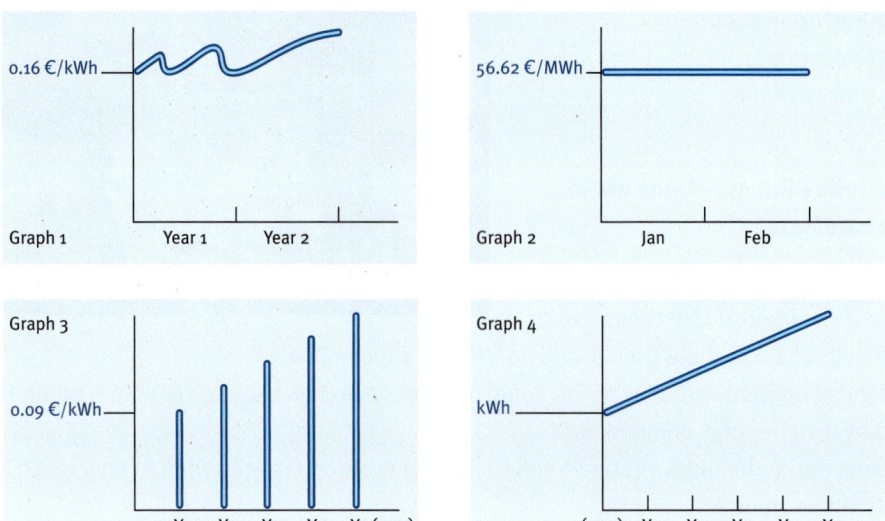

4 **Match the statements that have the same meaning. Then decide which graph each pair refers to.**

1 It's going to grow.
2 It has remained stable.
3 They've doubled.
4 It has fluctuated.

a It's held steady.
b It's been volatile.
c We expect it to rise.
d There's been a 100% increase.

5 **Which expression describes each trend shown? What other expressions do you know?**

decline • fall sharply • fluctuate • hit a low and then recover • increase steeply • level off • peak and then fall back • fall back and then pick up again • remain stable • rise steadily

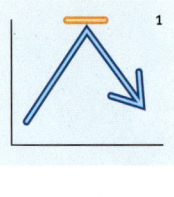

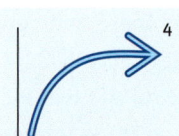

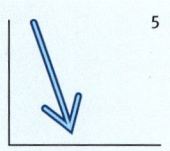

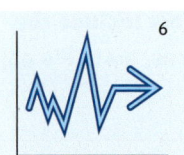

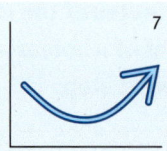

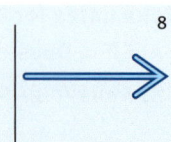

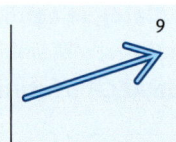

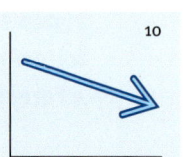

6 **This graph shows the development of the EEX electricity spot price in 2005. Continue the following description. Use expressions from exercises 4 and 5.**

'The graph shows the development of the EEX electricity spot price in 2005. The price started at ...'

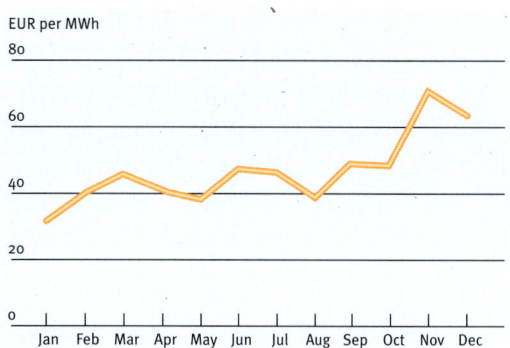

Choose a graph describing a trend from your own company on a subject that you are familiar with. Present it to the other students. Use phrases from the box.

DESCRIBING TRENDS, DEVELOPMENTS AND CONSEQUENCES

The graph shows ...
You can see here that ...
This happened/occurred because ...
We expected this change, but ...
Although there was a fall/rise ...

This led to ...
This resulted in ...
This was due to ...
This happened as a result of ...
This happened because of ...

---

7 **Write sentences describing developments and consequences using phrases from the right-hand column of the box.**

1 A surge in the gas price / harsh winter

_____

2 The economy picked up / increase in high-street spending

_____

3 A reduction in turnover / cost-cutting programme

_____

4 A power cut / collapse of the grid

_____

5 Consumers can choose their supplier / liberalization

_____

6 The volatile political situation / uncertainty in the market

_____

7 More wind farms have been built / financial support from the state

_____

_____

Now describe some developments and their consequences from your own company.

5

8 **AECP and ELEC (see exercise 2) signed a contract about energy supply. But then Anna Schmidt received a phone call. Listen and decide which four statements describe the situation.**

1 The weather has resulted in a crisis situation in the Netherlands.
2 The distribution network has gone down, but the transmission grid is unaffected.
3 The Dutch-German interconnector is out of action.
4 The problem has fortunately now been rectified.
5 Power is being fed in from France and Belgium.
6 There will be questions about liability and insurance.
7 AECP members may look for another supplier.

Complete this internal memo by Anna in a suitable way.

AECP crisis in Netherlands

Bad weather has disrupted supply to _____ . They are

_____, and operating on _____ generators at present.

_____ are working to resolve the situation, but AECP has brought up

the issue of _____ and is talking about _____ –

even though it's clearly a question of _____ .

> **VOCABULARY ASSISTANT**
> to disrupt *stören, unterbrechen*   to feed in *einspeisen*
> force majeure *höhere Gewalt*   interconnector *Verbundnetz*
> liability *Haftung*   to rectify *beheben*   to resolve *lösen*
> worrying *beunruhigend*

DID YOU KNOW?

UCTE stands for the Union for the Co-ordination of Transmission of Electricity. The members of this association are the transmission systems operators in continental Europe stretching from Spain through to Poland and Greece. It ensures the synchronous operation of interconnected power systems. A similar organization, Nordel, exists in the countries of Scandinavia.

9 **Match the expressions to the definitions.**

1 circuit breaker
2 force majeure
3 power outage
4 power surge
5 substation

a a unit which increases or decreases voltage levels
b a sharp, temporary rise in current or voltage levels which can cause damage to electrical equipment
c equipment which protects electrical apparatus from a sharp rise in current levels by switching off electrical current automatically
d loss of electrical power to an area
e an unexpected or uncontrollable event; nobody is at fault or responsible for subsequent damage

10   **Complete this letter of complaint from Paul Nieuwenhuis to Anna Schmidt with the expressions in the box.**

Before writing this letter • Dear Anna • He assured me • I look forward to hearing from you • I therefore suggest • May I remind you • I might add • We are extremely concerned • Yours sincerely

Association of European Chemical Producers

Energy Procurement Unit

Oranjeweg 118 • 3014 LA Rotterdam • Netherlands

Ms Anna Schmidt
ELEC International
Business Sales Unit
Hohewall 34
D-10423 Berlin
Germany

10 April 20..

_____ 1

I was somewhat dismayed to find out that just three weeks after I had signed the purchase contract with ELEC for our organization there was a sudden and complete breakdown in electricity supply to two of our members' production facilities in the Netherlands. _____ 2 that under the terms of our agreement ELEC is obliged to guarantee security of supply.

_____ 3 I spoke to one of ELEC´s engineers. He went into great technical detail about power surges and outages in the surrounding areas. _____ 4 that it was only due to our own circuit breakers that our plants were not severely damaged.

_____ 5 that his team was working around the clock to remedy the situation. He implied it was force majeure; this remains to be verified.

_____ 6 about the situation and are questioning whether ELEC can supply power to all our production locations throughout Europe.

_____ 7 we meet to discuss this most unfortunate state of affairs. I propose this meeting should take place at our headquarters in Rotterdam next week on Tuesday, April 17th at 10.00 am.

_____ 8.

_____ 9,

Dr. Paul Nieuwenhuis

Managing Director
AECP Energy Procurement Unit

11   **Write a reply to the letter on page 19 using phrases from the box below.**

> ### REPLYING TO LETTERS OF COMPLAINT
>
> I fully understand your concern, but …
> I would like to stress that …
> These are circumstances beyond our control.
> Nevertheless, …
>
> We are taking this matter very seriously.
> I would also like to assure you that …
> We are making every effort to …
> We are doing our utmost to …

If the crisis in the Netherlands happened to your company, how would it be resolved?

12   **Work with a partner to do this role-play.**

Paul phones Anna to talk about the agenda of their meeting. Prepare your roles and then role-play the telephone call. Use phrases for agreeing and disagreeing from page 8, and from the box below.

PARTNER FILES   Partner A   File 2, p. 56
Partner B   File 8, p. 57

> ### DEALING WITH A COMPLAINT
>
> **Giving assurance**
> I can assure you (that) …
> You have my assurance (that) …
> We're doing all we can to …
>
> **Sticking to a position**
> I really must insist (that) …
> Our position remains the same.
> Look, …
>
> **Strong disagreement**
> I can't accept that.
> That's not on.
> That's quite impossible.

13   **Discuss with a partner which statement describes the market your company operates in.**

1
In our country we have a very regulated market. We and our competitors have to comply with a lot of rules and regulations when doing business and it´s quite difficult to do things independently.

2
Our market is very liberalized. It's totally open to all players; companies offer gas and electricity at competitive prices to consumers and there is little state intervention.

Is there a lot of competition in your market? How difficult is it for new entrants to enter the market? What barriers do they face?

Switch off

How do power companies view organizations which look after consumers' interests? Read this Internet text about Energywatch in the UK and discuss the questions.

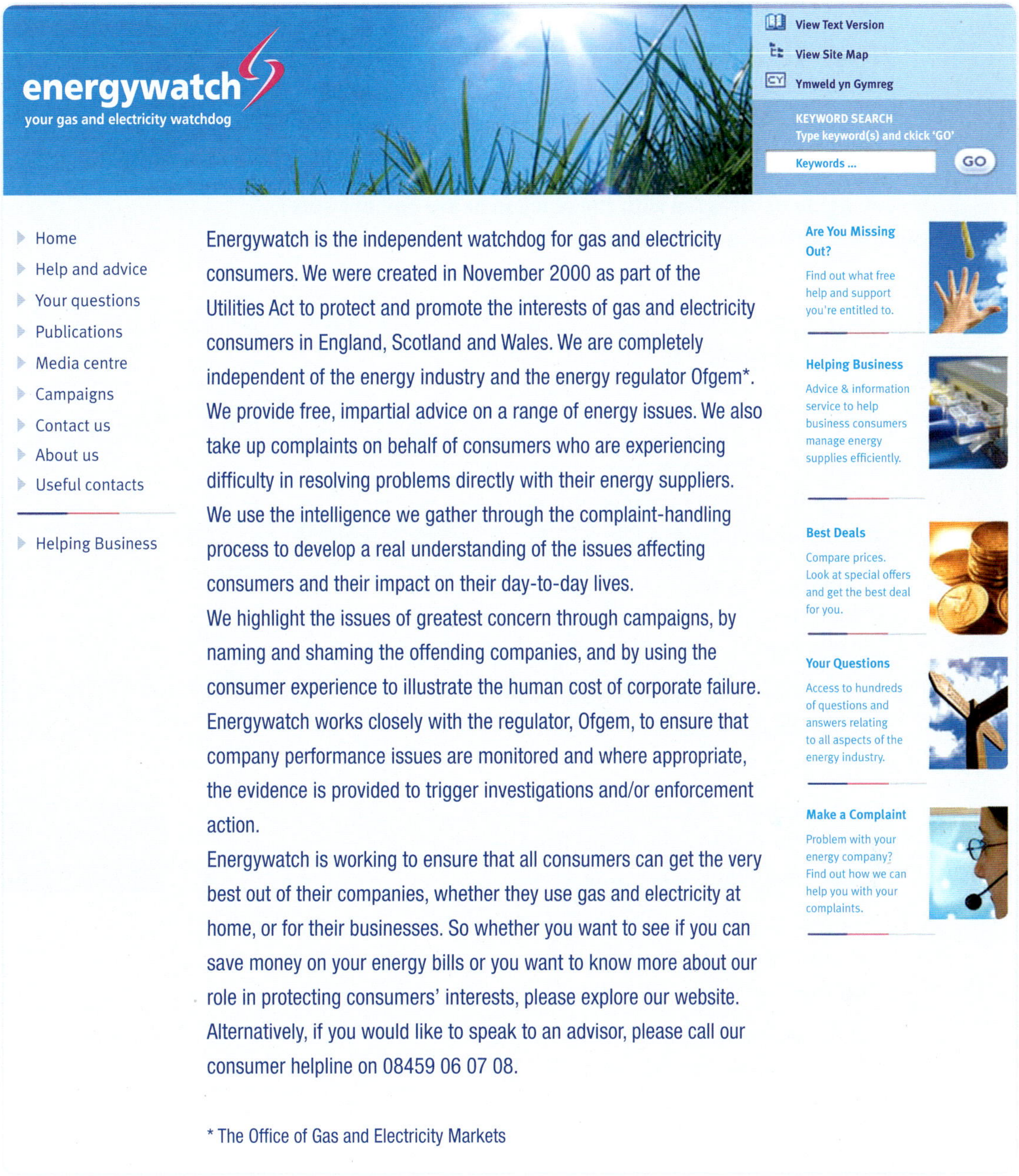

energywatch
your gas and electricity watchdog

View Text Version
View Site Map
Ymweld yn Gymreg

KEYWORD SEARCH
Type keyword(s) and ckick 'GO'
Keywords ... [GO]

- Home
- Help and advice
- Your questions
- Publications
- Media centre
- Campaigns
- Contact us
- About us
- Useful contacts

- Helping Business

Energywatch is the independent watchdog for gas and electricity consumers. We were created in November 2000 as part of the Utilities Act to protect and promote the interests of gas and electricity consumers in England, Scotland and Wales. We are completely independent of the energy industry and the energy regulator Ofgem*. We provide free, impartial advice on a range of energy issues. We also take up complaints on behalf of consumers who are experiencing difficulty in resolving problems directly with their energy suppliers. We use the intelligence we gather through the complaint-handling process to develop a real understanding of the issues affecting consumers and their impact on their day-to-day lives.

We highlight the issues of greatest concern through campaigns, by naming and shaming the offending companies, and by using the consumer experience to illustrate the human cost of corporate failure. Energywatch works closely with the regulator, Ofgem, to ensure that company performance issues are monitored and where appropriate, the evidence is provided to trigger investigations and/or enforcement action.

Energywatch is working to ensure that all consumers can get the very best out of their companies, whether they use gas and electricity at home, or for their businesses. So whether you want to see if you can save money on your energy bills or you want to know more about our role in protecting consumers' interests, please explore our website. Alternatively, if you would like to speak to an advisor, please call our consumer helpline on 08459 06 07 08.

* The Office of Gas and Electricity Markets

Are You Missing Out?
Find out what free help and support you're entitled to.

Helping Business
Advice & information service to help business consumers manage energy supplies efficiently.

Best Deals
Compare prices. Look at special offers and get the best deal for you.

Your Questions
Access to hundreds of questions and answers relating to all aspects of the energy industry.

Make a Complaint
Problem with your energy company? Find out how we can help you with your complaints.

Over to you

- Do you think such a watchdog agency is necessary? Give your reasons.
- How do such organizations influence the overall strategy and policy of energy companies?
- Are energy companies forced by legislation to cap prices in your country? If so, outline how this is done.
- Does the energy industry in your country have an organization which looks after the interests of power companies? If so, how does it do this?

3 Emissions and the environment

Switch on

Do you agree or disagree with these ideas or are you not sure? Discuss your answers with a partner.

	Agree	Disagree	Not sure
1 It's not necessary to educate people more on the issue of protecting the environment.	O	O	O
2 Cooking with gas is more environmentally-friendly than cooking with electricity.	O	O	O
3 Consumers should be obliged to buy only energy-saving electrical equipment.	O	O	O
4 Fossil fuel power plants should be totally replaced by ones using renewable sources.	O	O	O
5 A speed limit of 90 km/h should be established throughout the European Union to conserve oil stocks.	O	O	O
6 People should be encouraged to use public transport and not use their car.	O	O	O
7 All houses and buildings should be checked each year for their energy efficiency.	O	O	O
8 A massive green tax should be put on long-distance air travel to protect the environment.	O	O	O

VOCABULARY ASSISTANT

to encourage *ermutigen*
environment *Umwelt*
tax *Steuer*

A leaflet entitled 'Energy Saving Tips in the Home' is being developed. Write down your suggestions for tips and compare them with the rest of the class. Decide on the best ones.

1   Anna Schmidt at ELEC received this email invitation to a seminar. Complete the email with the expressions from the box.

by invitation only • Could you please let me know • I would also be grateful • It is with great pleasure • It would be beneficial • Kind regards • please see attachment • to get to know

Dear Anna,

_____[1] that we invite you to take part in the 10th "Induction Forum for Directors", an international management training seminar for department leaders who have recently been appointed. This three-day event will be taking place at the International Hotel in Geneva, Switzerland from May 5th to May 8th of this year (_____ _____[2] for more details).

Participation in this seminar is _____[3], and the main topic will be public relations regarding the image of ELEC and the energy industry as a whole, and how this image affects our business. The President and CEO of our company, Mrs Jane Hall, will be giving a talk on this subject. It will also give middle management the opportunity _____[4] her and the other members of the executive board.

_____[5] if you wish to attend this seminar by sending me an email.

_____[6] if you could inform me about any other issues you may wish to raise during these three days. There will be an open forum on Thursday evening, May 6th in which managers can discuss topics which they feel are important for the company. _____[7], however, if participants informed me about what they wish to discuss beforehand so that we can draw up a relevant agenda for the evening.

I look forward to hearing from you.

_____[8],

Sonia Lenoir

You are Anna. Write an answer to Sonia accepting the invitation. Ask her also to send the attachment again as it didn't come through to you. Tell her that in the open forum you would like to raise the issue of morale. Use phrases from the box to help you.

REPLYING TO INVITATIONS

Accepting invitations
I was delighted to receive your kind invitation …
Thank you very much for your kind invitation to take part in …
I would very much like to attend.

Making requests
Would/Could you please …?
I would be grateful if you could …
I would appreciate it if you could …

2 **Read this extract from a brochure created for the forum. Decide whether the statements that follow are true or false, and correct the false statements.**

Induction Forum for Directors

Dear Colleagues,

I am delighted to welcome you all to the 10th Induction Forum for Directors. The main focus of this event will be on how we, managers and employees alike, are ambassadors both for our company as well as our industry. We all need to be aware of the challenges that face us – particularly our image concerning the issue of the environment – and we all have to be more proactive regarding this matter.

On the face of it the statistics speak for themselves. 40% of our generating capacity is accounted for by lignite and coal, 25% by gas, 20% is attributable to nuclear energy, and just 15% accounted for by hydro and renewables. Our company is therefore seen by the public as one of the main culprits regarding climate change, air pollution, rising sea levels and other environmental problems including the hole in the ozone layer!

This is despite the fact that we have invested a lot of effort and money in finding solutions. All fossil fuel plants have been fitted with desulphurization plants to reduce emissions of greenhouse gases such as sulphur dioxide – one of the main causes of acid rain. We have also developed combustion technology to decrease carbon dioxide emissions, and we have installed denox equipment to reduce nitrogen oxides. We are also heavily involved in emissions trading.

There are many, particularly in the media and in politics, who would wish to highlight the negative aspects without even mentioning the measures that we have implemented over the last few years. This Forum will give us all the opportunity to discuss the issues and challenges so that we are able to respond in a professional and appropriate manner.

I am sure that we will have some very interesting and thought-provoking discussions.

Jane Hall
Chief Executive officer

1 People see ELEC as a 'clean' company.
2 Gas is the least important source in ELEC's energy mix.
3 Nuclear energy makes up 15% of generating capacity.
4 ELEC has invested a lot of money in technology to reduce emissions.
5 It is well known that the company has implemented a lot of measures to reduce emissions.
6 Managers have to be able to answer questions concerning ELEC's environment record.

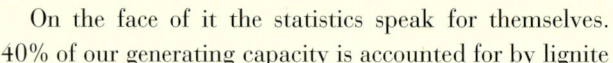

VOCABULARY ASSISTANT	combustion *Verbrennung* culprit *Übeltäter*
	desulphurization plant *Entschwefelungsanlage* nitrogen *Stickstoff*
	thought-provoking *zum Nachdenken anregend*

DID YOU KNOW?

The term 'manager' in the UK and USA covers a very broad range of positions. For example, a person who looks after customers could be called a 'Customer Care Manager' – even if the person's position is relatively low in the company hierarchy. Another person who leads a department could be called 'Department Manager'. In other languages the term has a more restricted meaning.

3 **Read Jane Hall's message again. Find expressions that fit into these sentences.**

1 The heating-up of the atmosphere is caused by _____ _____ .

2 The main cause of damage to trees is _____ _____ . It has been estimated that more than 60% of forests are affected.

3 The _____ in the _____ over the South Pole and Australia has raised levels of ultraviolet radiation. This can cause severe sunburn.

4 _____ _____ is one of the emissions from a power plant burning fossil fuels.

5 Winters are becoming milder and wetter, and average temperatures year-round are increasing. These are two major signs of _____ _____ .

6 Generators that pollute too much can buy credits or allowances from other companies in a system of _____ _____ .

7 The emitting of harmful gases into the atmosphere is called _____ _____ .

8 The Netherlands is in danger of being flooded due to a rise in _____ _____ .

9 A _____ _____ is the equipment in a power plant which removes sulphur dioxide.

6

4   **Listen to a presentation given by Jane Hall at the forum. In which order does she do the following?**

a   describe ELEC's present performance
b   invite questions
c   mention future plans for new plants
d   raise the issue of lobbying
e   welcome participants

Now complete this summary by one of the participants.

CEO Jane Hall's key point was the need to _____ at both a national and _____ level on the issues of _____ _____, so that all companies can _____ on the same basis.

> **VOCABULARY ASSISTANT**
>
> legislation   *Gesetzgebung*
> measure   *Maßnahme*
> pie chart   *Tortendiagramm*
> subsidy   *Subvention*

5   **Which of these phrases did Jane Hall use in her presentation? Listen again and check.**

> **GIVING A PRESENTATION**
>
> **Opening**
> Let me first introduce myself.
> I'm / My name is … .
> In this talk I want / would like to …
> I'll begin by (+ -ing form of verb).
> I'm going to be covering …
> Let's start with (+ noun).
>
> **Introducing other factors or points**
> If I could now turn to …
> Now, turning to …
> Let me move on to …
>
> **Introducing graphs and diagrams**
> I'd like you to look at this graph / diagram / (pie) chart / transparency / slide.
>
> **Comparing factors**
> First of all …
> Firstly …, secondly …, thirdly …
> On the one hand …, on the other hand …
>
> **Concluding**
> That completes my overview (of …).
> So, to summarize / sum up …
>
> **Questions**
> Please don't hesitate to interrupt me if you have any questions.
> If you have any questions, I'll be pleased to answer them at the end.
>
> **Finishing**
> Thank you for your attention.

Now prepare and give a short presentation on your job and the department in which you work. Use phrases from above.

7

6 Another speaker at the forum gives a talk on emissions trading and some research projects. Listen to what he says and make notes.

Emissions trading

_____

_____

_____

Imagine you are representing your company at an international conference. Explain in your own words how emissions trading works.

> **VOCABULARY ASSISTANT**
> to allocate *zuteilen*
> to emit *ausstoßen*
> to exceed *überschreiten*

7 At the conference you are asked the following questions. How would you answer?

1
How do you see the overall image of the energy industry in your country as regards environment protection?

2
How does the government in your country support protecting the environment? Are there any financial incentives?

3
What precisely does your company do to protect the environment? Do you have any schemes like carbon capture or designing CO2 neutral plants?

4
How great is the impact of emission control costs on the price of electricity?

5
Does the cost of protecting the environment have any repercussions on the competitiveness of your country's economy in world markets?

6
What programmes, if any, does the company you work for have to help customers save energy?

DID YOU KNOW?

As part of the UK's overall energy policy the Scottish Executive (government) has set a new target; 40% of all electricity generated in Scotland should come from renewable sources by 2020. This is not as far-fetched as it sounds as much of the land in Scotland is exposed to winds which are favourable for wind generation. The other option is to harness water or tidal energy; Scotland is a world leader in tidal research.

8 **Work in groups of three to do this role-play.**

At the seminar in Geneva, ELEC managers were asked to brainstorm ideas on how to improve the company's environmental image. Prepare your roles and then role-play the situation. Agree on a set of the best five proposals.

PARTNER FILES Partner A File 3, p. 56
Partner B File 9, p. 57
Partner C File 13, p. 58

9 **What do you think these newspaper articles are about? Write down the first paragraph. Then compare and discuss them with other members of the class.**

1 Europe to Cut Greenhouse Emissions by 20 %

2 **Wind Power Not Reliable**

3 **Environment Protection Costs Jobs**

4 The First Step to Improve Your Carbon Footprint

5 **Global Warming –** All the Fault of Energy Companies

6 Green Tax for Air Travel and Generators

7 Coal Industry to Pay for CO_2 Emissions

10 **There are a lot of acronyms and abbreviations used in the energy industry. What do the following stand for, and in which context are they used (eg generation, emissions, etc)?**

1 CO2
2 SO2
3 CHP
4 V
5 UCTE
6 TSO
7 DSO
8 MW
9 kWh

11 **Complete this puzzle and find an essential function for most companies. What is the word in column a? The answers are all words from this unit.**

1 What you do when you take and store a substance for a long period. You do it with carbon dioxide, for example, and pump it into the ground.
2 the type of gases which warm the earth's atmosphere
3 financial support from the state usually for industrial purposes
4 energy sources such as wind, the sun, etc
5 a diagram with a horizontal and vertical axis
6 the first element in CO2
7 the type of rain produced by some emissions from power stations and which badly affects trees
8 to alter something or to make something different

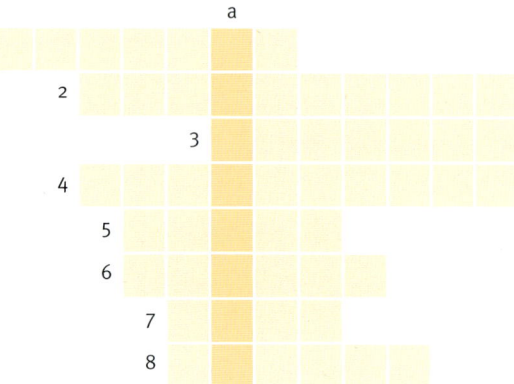

Switch off

Which organization makes sure that emission limits are observed in your country?
Read this newspaper article about the Kyoto Protocol and discuss the questions.

The Kyoto Protocol

The Kyoto Protocol is the name of an international treaty to reduce the amount of greenhouse-gas emissions which came into effect in 2005. The signatories of this binding agreement are divided into two categories, so-called "Annex 1" and "Non-Annex 1" countries. The former comprises developed countries which made a commitment to

cut greenhouse-gas emissions to 5% below 1990 levels by 2008–2012. Under the terms of the agreement, the latter had no actual mandatory greenhouse emission restrictions, but were to be able to sell carbon credits on the international market to Annex 1 buyers as part of any emission-reduction project implemented in these countries. This was to be on a voluntary basis.

A number of countries did not ratify the treaty, notably the USA – the largest emitter of greenhouse gases – and (initially) Australia. In addition, India and China, which have large populations and rapidly expanding economies, did not set emission limits, at least not under the terms of the Protocol. This was justified by the fact that these countries were not the main contributors of emissions during the process of the world's industrialization period ie the 19th and 20th centuries.

This brought the whole project into doubt in terms of reaching the targets envisaged. Indeed, some critics called the Kyoto Protocol flawed because in their view it favoured some countries at the expense of others. Others said that the treaty should only be seen as a first step to manage greenhouse emissions on a global scale, and that stricter measures and limits should be implemented as soon as possible, which should be adopted by all countries not just the developed ones.

Since the Protocol came into force, the majority of politicians, economists and environmentalists have reached the view that if nothing is done to address climate change we will be heading for economic, social and environmental collapse throughout the world.

Over to you

- What do you think of the Kyoto Protocol? Did it set attainable goals?
- Are industrialized countries to blame for climate change? What about the position of energy companies?
- What about the position of China and India? Is it fair? Why (not)?

4 The nuclear issue

Switch on

What words do you associate with nuclear energy? Complete the diagram below, then compare and discuss your diagram with other members of your class.

Waste

NUCLEAR POWER

Health

Security

1   How much do you know about nuclear energy? Work with a partner and complete this quiz.

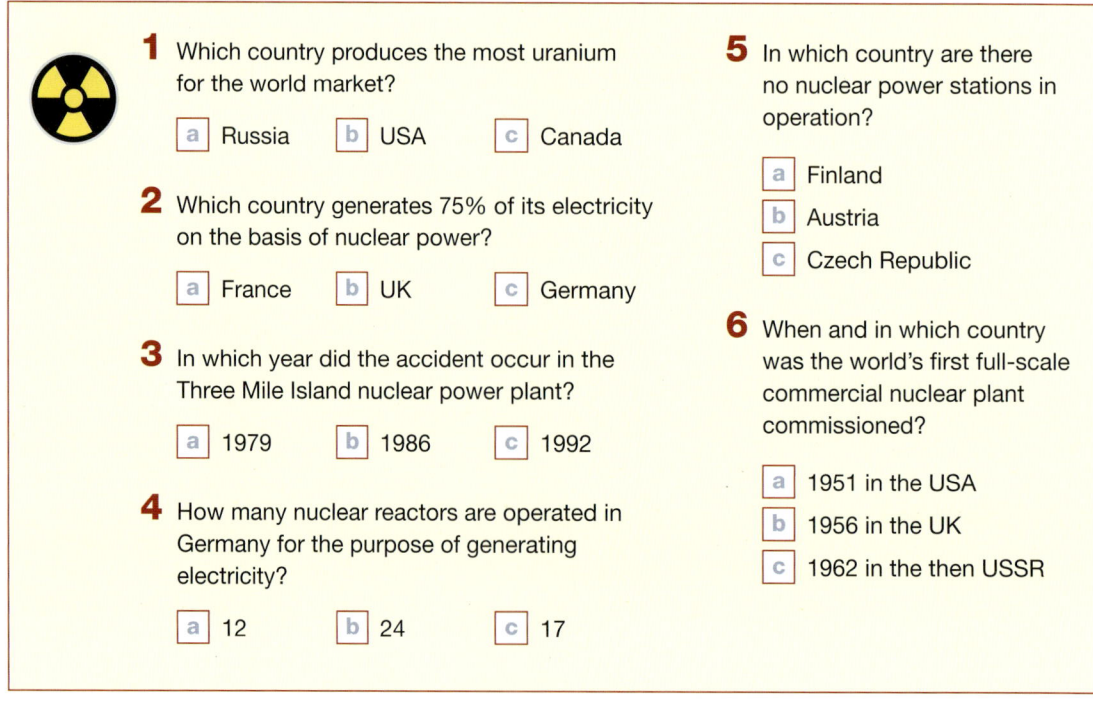

1 Which country produces the most uranium for the world market?

a Russia   b USA   c Canada

2 Which country generates 75% of its electricity on the basis of nuclear power?

a France   b UK   c Germany

3 In which year did the accident occur in the Three Mile Island nuclear power plant?

a 1979   b 1986   c 1992

4 How many nuclear reactors are operated in Germany for the purpose of generating electricity?

a 12   b 24   c 17

5 In which country are there no nuclear power stations in operation?

a Finland
b Austria
c Czech Republic

6 When and in which country was the world's first full-scale commercial nuclear plant commissioned?

a 1951 in the USA
b 1956 in the UK
c 1962 in the then USSR

Now discuss these questions briefly in your group.

1   Is the image of nuclear power in your country generally positive or negative? Give some details.
2   Are new plants being built? If so, outline where this is being done.
3   Is nuclear power being phased out? If so, outline the reasons.
4   Are nuclear plants economically viable when compared with other types of power stations? State what you think.
5   What is the situation in your country concerning the storage and disposal of nuclear waste?

DID YOU KNOW?

The very first time that electricity was generated using a nuclear reactor was in 1951 at an experimental power plant near Arco, Idaho in the USA.

---

2   **Uranium is the basis of nuclear energy. Work with a partner and put these sentences in the correct order so that they describe the processes the uranium goes through.**

☐   a   After that, the uranium ore is crushed into a fine powder.
☐   b   First of all, uranium is extracted from opencast or underground mining.
☐   c   The next step is fuel fabrication. The nuclear fuel is transformed into pellets.
☐   d   This yellow cake is then enriched to increase the proportion of uranium 235, which is essential in the nuclear fission process.
☐   e   Finally, the spent fuel must be reprocessed and stored long term underground.
☐   f   Following that, they are formed into rods and placed in the reactor pressure vessel.
☐   g   In the reactor pressure vessel heat is produced through a fissile reaction and eventually the uranium is used up.
☐   h   After crushing, the powder is then purified; the substance at the end of this process is called 'yellow cake'.

VOCABULARY ASSISTANT
to enrich *anreichern*
to extract *fördern*
ore *Erz*   pellets *Granulat*
to reprocess *wiederaufbereiten*

3 **A group of international visitors is being shown round a nuclear power plant. Listen to this talk on its operation and label the diagram.**

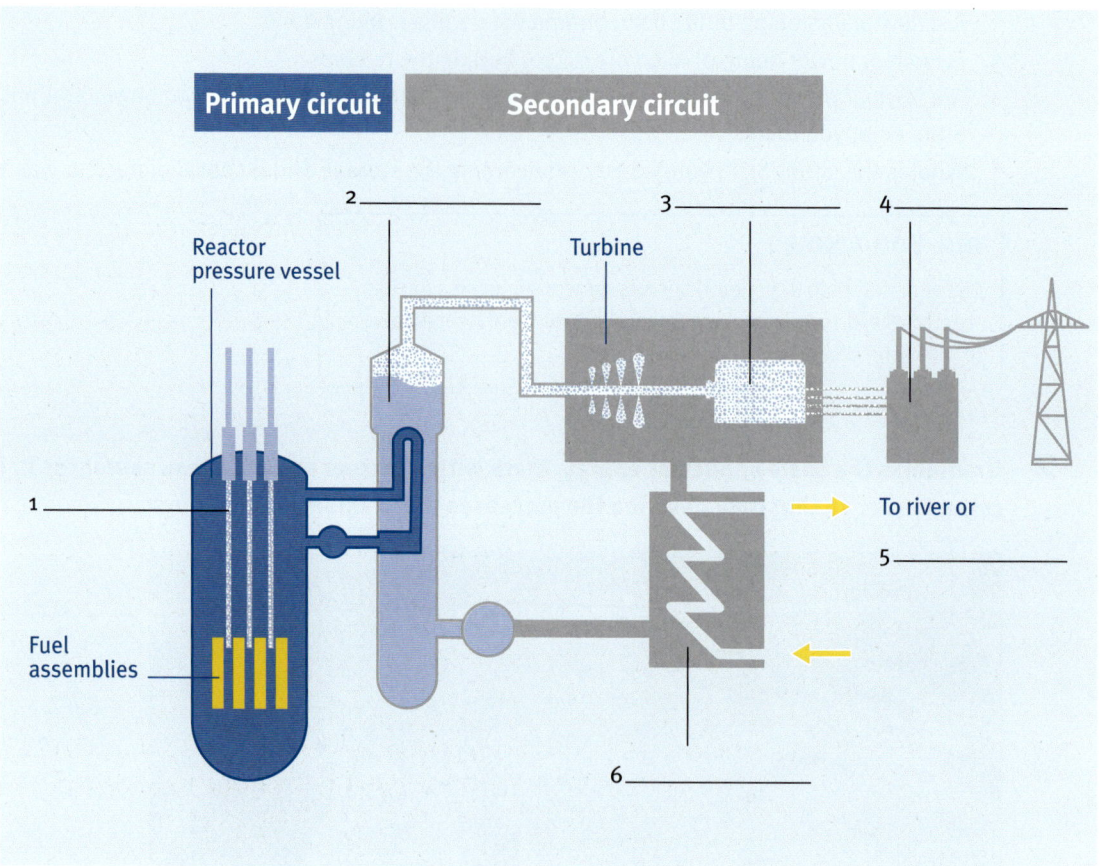

Listen again and take notes on the purpose and functions of these parts of the power station. You need the notes for exercise 4.

1   The reactor pressure vessel
2   The primary circuit
3   The steam generator
4   The transformers
5   The condenser

4 **Put yourself in the position of the guide in exercise 3. Use the diagram, your notes, and phrases from below to describe the whole process in your own words.**

> **DESCRIBING A PROCESS**
>
> Firstly / First of all …   Following that …
> After that …   Finally …
> The next step/stage is …   The final step …
> Then …

5   **Read and order these sentences from a publicity brochure describing the process of waste disposal. Link the sentences with phrases from above.**

a   _____ the spent fuel rods are extracted from the reactor.

b   _____ the waste needs to be buried deep underground in a safe location.

c   Eventually the spent fuel has to be reprocessed, so _____ that it is transported to a reprocessing plant, such as Sellafield in the UK and La Hague in France. There it is vitrified and sealed in steel canisters.

d   _____ the waste is transferred to a site where interim storage is possible. There are a number of such sites in Europe.

Reactor	→	Interim storage	→	Reprocessing plant	→	Final storage

VOCABULARY ASSISTANT
to seal *versiegeln*
spent *abgebrannt*
to vitrify *zu Glas schmelzen*

6   **A work-group at ELEC is discussing the issue of waste disposal in order to formulate a new public relations strategy. You have the task of taking notes. Listen and note down the key issues.**

Storage and reprocessing
_____
_____
_____
_____
_____

Long-term disposal
_____
_____
_____
_____

VOCABULARY ASSISTANT
to adhere to something *etwas einhalten*
clay *Lehm*   to dispose of something *etwas entsorgen*   legislation *Gesetzgebung*   rundown *Zusammenfassung*   storage *Lager*

7   **Match the words to make expressions from the discussion in exercise 6. Listen again if necessary.**

1 public	a measures
2 government	b storage
3 disposal	c plants
4 spent	d fuel
5 safety	e facility
6 reprocessing	f resistance
7 interim	g disposal
8 waste	h legislation

Now complete these sentences using the correct expression.

9   Companies which operate nuclear power plants must have a programme for _____

_____ so that unwanted products can be dealt with safely.

10   There are facilities for _____ at nuclear power stations to store waste for a limited time until a permanent location can be found.

11   _____ is the uranium which has been used up.

12   The two most well-known _____ in Europe are Sellafield in the UK and La Hague in France.

13   Waste can be stored in a _____.

14   There is a lot of _____ to nuclear power; some people just don't like it.

15   Other members of the public are not convinced of the _____ _____ at nuclear power stations, and think radiation will leak into the atmosphere.

16   Many people have no trust in the politicians who draft new _____ _____ regarding nuclear power.

8   **ELEC has been sent a report produced by a firm of consultants, Finley Consultants. Read this excerpt. What problem do the consultants see and what solution do they propose?**

Each country within the European Union has its own policy on nuclear power, which makes it very difficult for European generators to plan effectively for the future. Some countries wish to phase out nuclear power plants altogether. This would have an adverse effect on jobs, and also diminish Europe's reputation as a location for nuclear technology.

It is suggested that what is needed is a new strategy. A uniform approach is required through which both national governments and the European Commission can be lobbied. Efforts need to be consolidated so that all lobbyists in Brussels and other European capitals are pulling in the same direction. New legislation, or amendments to current laws, should be geared towards the interests of both European energy supply and the industry at large.

ELECs Jane Hall has requested a response to Finley Consultants' report from managers. Write her an email and include the following points.

1   You don't think the EU will ever have a uniform policy.
2   ELEC should nevertheless support the call.
3   Agree with the consultants on the question of jobs and expertise.
4   Some countries have reversed their decision to phase out nuclear power (eg Finland, Sweden). Say how this may affect developments.
5   Suggest a meeting with lobbyists from ELEC and its competitors to form strategy.

9   **Mary Brown, Jane Hall's secretary, phones Jacques Royale of the strategy unit to set up a time for a meeting to discuss the proposals made by Finley Consultants. Put the dialogue into the correct order.**

☐	a	*Jacques*	Hello. Jacques Royale speaking.
☐	b	*Mary*	Ok, how about Tuesday, March 6th at 3 pm?
☐	c	*Jacques*	I could make four. Could you change it to 4 pm?
☐	d	*Mary*	Hello, Jacques. Mary Brown here.
☐	e	*Jacques*	Let me check my diary. I'm afraid that's not so good as I've got a meeting with some members of the supervisory board most of Monday morning.
☐	f	*Mary*	Yes, that's fine, four is also OK. I'll send everybody a quick email to confirm everything.
☐	g	*Jacques*	Hi Mary. What can I do for you?
☐	h	*Mary*	Yes. Bye, Jacques.
☐	i	*Jacques*	Great. Well, I'll probably see you next week.
☐	j	*Mary*	I'm phoning to set up a meeting between the board and the strategy unit to discuss the proposals made by Finley Consultants. Would next Monday at 9 am suit you?
☐	k	*Jacques*	Bye.

10   **The strategy unit has prepared a list of arguments for maintaining nuclear power. Work with a partner and rate them on a scale of 1–3 (1 = very important, 2 = important, 3 = not important). Then discuss results in the class.**

Nuclear power should be maintained because	Rating
1 it safeguards jobs in the power industry.	☐
2 it preserves expertise in nuclear technology.	☐
3 it is difficult to replace the high proportion of power generated from nuclear fuel.	☐
4 it reduces dependency on the import of fossil fuels from politically unstable countries.	☐
5 the targets of the Kyoto Protocol will not be met if nuclear power is phased out.	☐
6 the phasing out of nuclear power is pointless as the waste produced from the past still has to be disposed of.	☐
7 it can be used as a 'bridge' until new technologies are developed in the future.	☐
8 the economy would go into recession without it because the kWh price would increase.	☐
9 the world market price of uranium is not as volatile as other fuels.	☐
10 the cost of decommissioning and dismantling plants is far too high even if energy companies have provisions for this purpose.	☐

Look at two or three websites of the main energy companies in your country. What PR information on nuclear power do they offer? What could you add to the list above? How does your company communicate with opponents to nuclear power?

> **VOCABULARY ASSISTANT**
>
> to decommission *außer Betrieb nehmen*
> provisions *Rückstellungen*

11   **Work with a partner. What counter-arguments can you think of to each of those in exercise 10? The first one is given as an example. Compare and discuss your counter-arguments with the rest of the class.**

1   Other jobs could be created if more money were invested in renewables.

2   _____

3   _____

4   _____

5   _____

6   _____

7   _____

8   _____

9   _____

10 _____

12 Work in groups of three to do this role-play.

One outcome of the strategy meeting was a decision to set up training seminars aimed at helping employees respond to opponents of nuclear power. At one of the seminars employees role-play a meeting between a chairperson (Partner A), an environmentalist (Partner B) and a representative of the energy industry (Partner C). Prepare your roles and act out the role-play.

PARTNER FILES
Partner A   File 4, p. 56
Partner B   File 10, p. 57
Partner C   File 14, p. 58

CHAIRING A MEETING

Opening the meeting
First of all, I think we should establish the overall procedure.
Can we now agree on the overall procedure?
The main objectives of the meeting are …
Does that seem acceptable to you?

Asking somebody to start
Would you like to start, John?
John, would you like to kick off?

Keeping to the agenda
OK, could we please come back to the agenda?
I'm afraid that's not part of the discussion.

Asking for clarification
I don't quite follow. What do you mean by …?
I don't really get what you mean.

---

13 Complete this puzzle and find the word in column a.

1 A short-term, temporary, not permanent solution is an … solution.
2 When you take a fossil fuel or ore from a mine, you … it.
3 Getting rid of waste or putting it in storage is waste …
4 the primary fuel used in nuclear power
5 When you stop something gradually over a period, you … it …
6 This is the place in the plant where nuclear fission takes place.
7 an expression which means 'to comply with', for example, a law or regulation
8 We use this word to describe nuclear fuel which has been used up.
9 to decommission a plant and take it apart carefully piece by piece

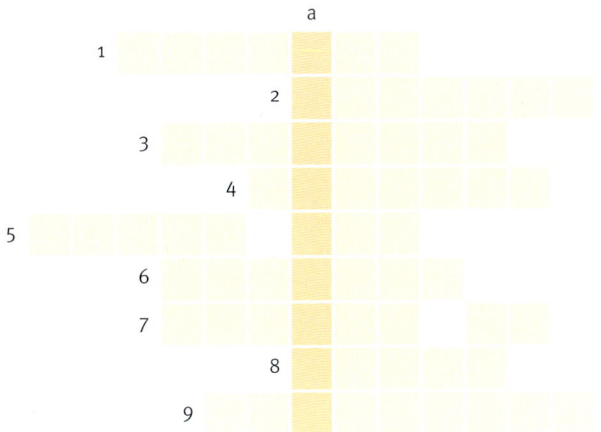

DID YOU KNOW?

The International Atomic Energy Authority (IAEA) was established in 1957 and around 140 states are members of this organization. Its main function is to promote safe, secure and peaceful use of nuclear technologies throughout the world.

Switch off

How do you see the future of nuclear power? Read this newspaper article about nuclear fusion and discuss the questions.

Nuclear Fusion – the Way Forward?

The challenge for the nuclear power industry is to make the technology as safe and secure as possible. After all, most people have heard of the catastrophic effects of the accident at Chernobyl in 1986 – the repercussions of which can still be seen today, with radioactive fallout

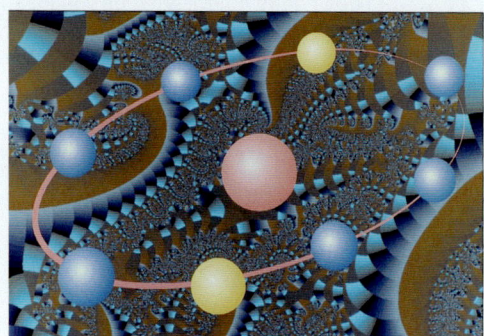

contaminating large areas of Ukraine, Russia and Belarus. There is also the contentious issue of dealing with the waste from the nuclear fission process, which has still not been adequately dealt with in most countries.

The question arises: can such waste be avoided in the first place? Not it would seem with nuclear fission, but nuclear fusion could be the answer if it is ever successfully developed.

In this process isotopes of hydrogen – deuterium and tritium – have to be heated up to over 100 million °C. The atoms are thereby fused together thus releasing enormous amounts of thermal energy, which could then be harnessed to produce electricity. There are a number of benefits. No greenhouse gases are released, very little radioactive waste is produced – as is the case with nuclear fission – and furthermore the primary fuel is abundantly available on earth.

This technology, however, is still in its infancy. The EU, USA, China, India, Russia, Japan and South Korea have set up a project called ITER (the International Thermonuclear Experimental Reactor), which includes an experimental reactor in Cadarache, France. The goal of the project is to make fusion commercially viable. But experts say it will take at least thirty years to achieve the target and there is also no guarantee of any success.

ITER has other critics too. Some environmental groups claim that the money invested in the project – around €10 billion – should be used to develop renewable energy, firstly because it is available today and secondly because it has a proven track record. ■

Over to you

- Do you think nuclear fusion can be developed successfully? State your reasons.
- Should countries cooperate to develop new technologies concerning energy production? Give your reasons why or why not.
- Do you think the money invested in the ITER project should be spent elsewhere?
- Do you agree that renewables have a proven track record?

Investment plans

Switch on

What factors do managers of energy companies take into account when considering a takeover? Complete the diagram, then compare and discuss your diagram with other members of your class.

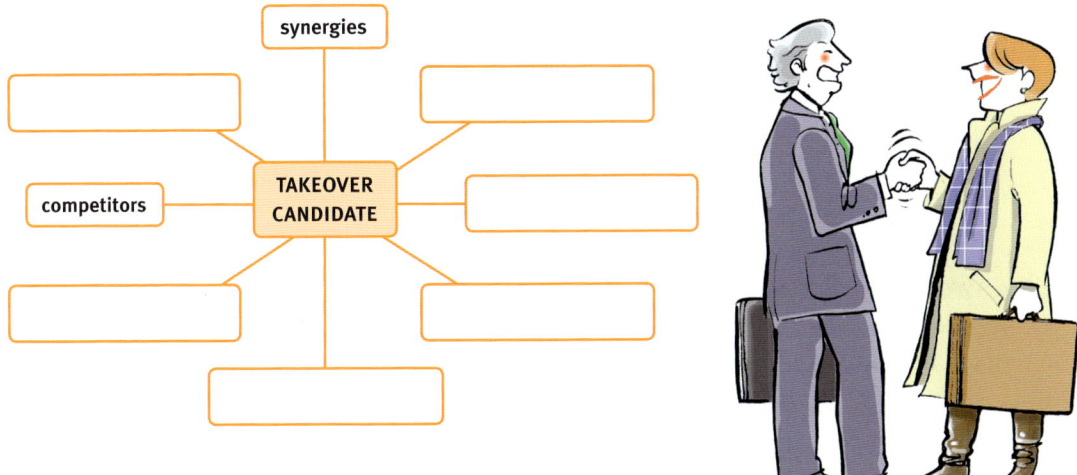

- synergies
- competitors

TAKEOVER CANDIDATE

**What mergers or acquisitions do you know about?
How successful were they and what were the consequences?**

10

1 **ELEC is making a takeover bid for the Scottish company, Strathclyde Energy. ELEC's PR department is monitoring the media coverage. Listen to this radio report and take notes on reactions to the bid from these four (groups of) people.**

1 consumers
2 staff
3 the British Trade and Industry minister, Hilary Alexander
4 financial analysts

VOCABULARY ASSISTANT
assurance *Zusicherung*
redundancy *betriebsbedingte Kündigung*
takeover *Übernahme* viable *rentabel*

2   **Complete the sentences below from the radio report. Listen again to check your answers.**

1   A lot of people will be _____ to other companies if a price increase occurs.

2   Staff in the company are deeply concerned about _____ .

3   There have been _____ made by ELEC that staff have nothing to fear.

4   The Trade and Industry Minister, Hilary Alexander, is also making sure that everything is

_____ .

5   She fears the move may _____ European competition laws.

6   It's just not _____ that large firms from abroad buy British firms.

7   Some analysts claim that the potential for _____ within a new corporate structure would be minimal.

8   They doubt whether the takeover would be a viable _____ .

9   The company is already having dificulties _____ its interests in Spain with its operations in the rest of Europe.

3   **A SWOT analysis helps a company to identify its internal strengths and weaknesses, and its external opportunities and threats. Before the takeover bid managers at Strathclyde listed these 13 points about their firm. Sort them into the SWOT matrix.**

SWOT Analysis	
Strengths	Weaknesses
Opportunities	Threats

Now work with a partner and decide how you see your company's strengths, weaknesses, opportunities and threats. Present your findings to the rest of the class.

Items for SWOT analysis

1   Profit levels currently healthy

2   Staff morale satisfactory

3   Management structure hierarchical: means decision-making process slow

4   Good customer service, but high prices

5   Legislation from Brussels could impair operations.

6   Other companies are penetrating traditional markets.

7   Plans to take over one competitor; synergy effects possible

8   Number of employees relatively high for business; could be reduced

9   Core business electricity and gas

10   Gas distribution grid in need of repair

11   Good chances of further penetrating UK market

12   Regulator is monitoring company's presence in local geographical area.

13   Due to profit levels, the company could become a takeover candidate.

DID YOU KNOW?

British managers can appear to be quite open with little evidence of hierarchy and with the focus of meetings being made on teamwork. For outsiders this can be misleading as the decision-making process can be quite slow in reality. Most senior managers will probably have the final say although there still may be a period of building up consensus within the group during a meeting.

3 **News of the takeover bid produced familiar reactions. Read these statements and decide who is in favour, who is against, and who is neutral.**

2
Takeovers and mergers in any industry are necessary for consolidation and investment. They enhance efficiency in the market, and uncompetitive utilities will go out of business anyway.

1
If you look at takeovers and mergers in the energy business it's always the same old story. Managers talk about shareholder value with little concern for employees who will be laid off or encouraged to take early retirement.

3
At the end of the day what do we see? Top managers get bonuses and other benefits while the consumer just gets higher prices. I think it's all bad for competition within the energy market.

6
The real problem is collusion and uncompetitive pricing. It's essential that there is the right legislation in place to stop such things. It doesn't really matter whether companies are owned and run privately or by the state.

4
Every country has an authority to prevent the bigger electricity and gas companies from abusing their position. And anyway, an energy company from one European country is free to merge with or takeover a firm in another.

5
To be honest, I'd like Europe to return to the old set-up. Each country had one or two monopolistic utilities that really looked after all stakeholders – especially the employees and the customers.

Now say which statements you agree with and why.

VOCABULARY ASSISTANT

to abuse *missbrauchen*
collusion *geheime Absprache*
to lay off *entlassen*

5 **Before ELEC took over Strathclyde Energy, financial statements were analysed. Match these documents to their definitions.**

☐ 1 Balance sheet

☐ 2 Profit and loss account (income statement)

☐ 3 Cash flow statement

a This statement shows the expenditures and sales of a company over a period of time. These are balanced to give a final positive or negative figure.

b Basically a statement which shows incoming and outgoing cash of a company during a particular period.

c This document gives details about the financial position of a company at a particular time. It is divided into assets, equity and liabilities.

A balance sheet lists fixed assets, current assets, equity, and liabilities. Work with a partner and sort the following terms into these four categories.

accounts payable (money the company owes to its suppliers) • accounts receivable (money owed to the company by its customers) • buildings • cash at the bank • company capital (owned by shareholders) • inventory • long-term financial assets • power plants • provisions

VOCABULARY ASSISTANT	
current assets	*Umlaufvermögen*
equity	*Aktienkapital*
fixed assets	*Anlagevermögen*
liabilities	*Verbindlichkeiten*

6 **Look at a copy of the most recently issued balance sheet of the company you work for (from the last annual report or the Internet). Answer these questions.**

1 What fixed assets does your company have? What does the company use them for?

2 Has the value of these fixed assets gone down compared with the previous year? If so, explain why. Is it due to depreciation or to other reasons?

3 What are your company's current assets?

4 What do the inventories of the company consist of? What are they used for?

5 What is the value of your company's equity? Who owns the shares?

6 What are the provisions in your company used for?

7 Why is it important to have the provisions?

DID YOU KNOW?

ROI stands for return on investment. It is a ratio that measures the profit gained relative to the amount of money invested. It is usually expressed as a percentage and gives an indication whether a particular investment is meeting expectations.

7 **After the takeover has gone through, Richard Mellor receives a phone call from his ELEC colleague, Anna. Listen to the phone call. What does Richard have to note down in his calendar?**

Now listen again for the details. Answer these questions.

1 What concrete plan has Anna been given the task of implementing?
2 What will be the consequences for staff in Scotland?
3 How urgent is it to take action?
4 What's on her agenda?
5 Why does she want the meeting in Germany rather than in Scotland?

VOCABULARY ASSISTANT	to jeopardize *gefährden* to retain *(weiter)beschäftigen* trade union *Gewerkschaft*

8 **Work in a group of three to do this role-play.**

Anna (Partner A), Richard (Partner B) and James Sinclair (Partner C) meet in Berlin. Prepare your roles and act out the role-play. Your task is to agree on a strategy.

PARTNER FILES
Partner A   File 5, p. 56
Partner B   File 11, p. 57
Partner C   File 15, p. 58

DISCUSSION IN A MEETING

Proposing
Couldn't we just …?
What if we …?
Why don't we …?

Asking for agreement/disagreement
Do we all agree on that?
Does anybody object to this?
Who's in favour of this proposal?

Showing concern
I have some reservations/concerns about …
Actually, I don't think that's a good idea.

Emphasizing
I'd again like to point out that …
I know I keep going on about this, but …

9 **Your company is following developments at ELEC closely. You find this information. Write a memo summarizing ELEC's plans.**

Mixed reactions to Yorkshire plans

ELEC, the European energy group, has just announced plans to develop new coal fields in Yorkshire, England, together with the construction a new coal-fired plant. This move has puzzled industrial analysts as it is well known that coal production is more expensive in industrialized countries than other parts of the world, mainly because of higher labour costs.

It is even more surprising given the present glut of coal on the world market and that British Coal withdrew from the area in 1990 saying that mining was no longer viable. ELEC, however, is confident that the project is a viable investment. It has forecast that the present situation will change and also stressed the fact that personnel costs in the UK are among the lowest in Western Europe. The company also maintains that it can mine coal more efficiently because of advances in extraction technology. In addition, oil and gas prices are set to soar.

What do you think of the plan? Could it be a viable investment? Why (not)?

10 **ELEC opened a visitor centre in Yorkshire. The centre had this diagram of a coal-fired plant. Complete the gaps using the words from the box, then describe the processes at the plant in your own words. Use phrases for describing a process in Unit 4, page 32.**

Functional diagram of power plant process

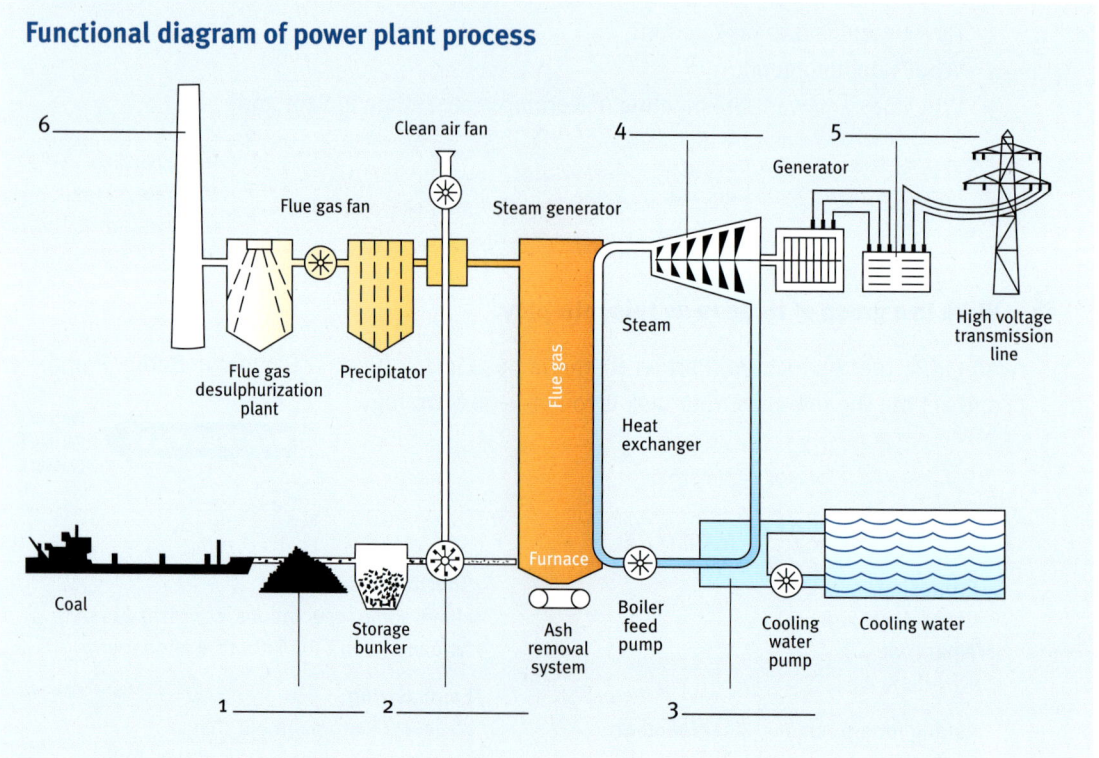

coal crusher • coal storage area • condenser • stack • transformer • turbine

11   These headlines are taken from energy journals. Write down the first paragraph of each article and then compare and discuss your texts with other members of the class.

> 1   **New State-of-the-Art Plant Creates 50 New Jobs**

> 2   **Energy Firms Swallow Up Municipal Utilities.**

> 3   **Coal Makes a Comeback**

> 4   **Too Much Red Tape Stifles Investment**

Now work with a partner and find out about one of your company's investment projects from the firm's website, annual report or other sources. Present your results to the rest of the class.

Switch off

Why do energy companies disinvest and/or sell off operations? Read this newspaper article about disinvestment and discuss the questions.

 # Disinvestment in Europe

In a due diligence process a company wishing to take over another firm would carefully investigate all the facts and aspects of the deal before making a final decision. In the energy business one important issue is whether the operations of a takeover candidate actually correspond to the core business of the buying company. This is not as straightforward as it may seem. Some candidates may have operations covering public transport or water supply. Subsequent investment must be contemplated as sometimes the infrastructures such as the water-pipe systems or vehicles may need replacing or repair. Unwanted activities could be sold off or disinvested after the takeover, but this may not always be possible or the procedures may prove to be too cumbersome.

This aspect of disinvestment is not to be underestimated. European energy companies may have to take on the mighty European Commission when drawing up their investment plans as there are moves to force companies to unbundle their divisions completely. For those involved in generation, transport and supply, it would mean selling off transmission and distribution networks to new owners and operators. All for the sake of market liberalization and transparency it is said. Others claim it is tantamount to expropriation.

But who would invest in these girds? Some in Brussels say the taxpayer. But this would be nationalization through the backdoor, which would make a mockery of free-market policies in Europe.

Over to you

- Do you think the European Commission is right to force energy companies to sell off their grids? State your reasons.
- How does the government in your country view this?
- Do you agree with the concept of nationalization? Is it good for stakeholders (shareholders, employees and customers)?

6 The future of energy

Switch on

How do you see the future? Look at the points given below and note down how you see developments over the next five years. Compare and discuss your ideas with other members of the class.

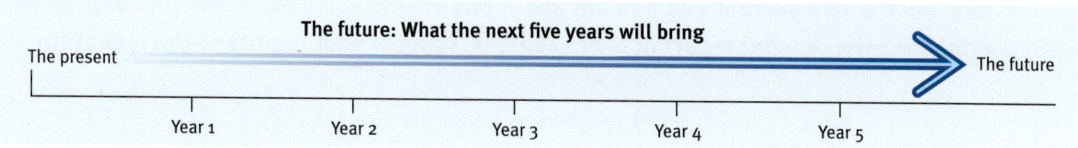

The future: What the next five years will bring

The present ———————————————————————————→ The future

Year 1   Year 2   Year 3   Year 4   Year 5

1 your own job responsibilities
2 the functions of the department you work in
3 the projections for your company's market(s)
4 the communication flow within your company
5 pay and conditions of the staff at your company
6 the core business of your firm
7 your company's image
8 innovations created or used by your company
9 the structure of your company

1 What are the functions of the departments listed below? Match the targets to the departments.

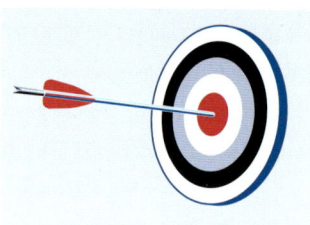

Departments
1 auditing
2 human resources
3 IT
4 legal services
5 public relations (PR)
6 procurement
7 research and development (R&D)
8 sales and marketing

Targets
a to acquire more industrial customers
b to be more proactive about negative media coverage
c to bundle purchase volume
d to develop a sustainable sponsorship strategy for sport and cultural events
e to establish a computer helpline for staff
f to establish benchmarks or yardsticks for an interdepartmental costing system
g to harmonize pension schemes throughout the group
h to identify inefficiencies in financial processes
i to implement new payroll processes
j to make tests in fuel-cell technology
k to reduce the number of suppliers
l to set up a loyalty-card system for retail customers
m to standardize contracts
n to upgrade software

> **VOCABULARY ASSISTANT**
> benchmark *Maßstab*
> fuel cell *Brennstoffzelle*
> payroll *Gehaltsabrechnung*
> sustainable *nachhaltig*   yardstick *Maßstab*

2   Read the following email from a manager. Does Jan work in the procurement, trading or auditing department?

> I am going to meet the CEO shortly as she has expressed concerns that we are still having some problems regarding accurate load planning. The accuracy of our forecasts for last year was disappointing. I would appreciate it if you could inform me of the reasons as you see them.
>
> Regards,
>
> Jan Balkenende

Now answer the email. Include the following points and use the expressions from the box. Each expression should be used once only.

attributable to • I am afraid • in addition • over and above • to begin with

1   Agree that forecasting was disappointing.
2   There was a sharp rise in consumption due to an unexpected economic upswing.
3   One power plant went out of action because of technical problems.
4   The Dutch/German interconnector was damaged at the beginning of the year.
5   Communication between departments must also be improved.

3   At an interdepartmental meeting, ELEC employees are discussing the future of energy supply. Listen and take notes for the minutes using the headings below.

12

Issues discussed

1 Long-distance electricity transmission

_____

2 R&D department project

_____

3 Geothermal heating

_____

4 Hydrogen

_____

_____

Do you agree with the points made? Give your reasons.

> **VOCABULARY ASSISTANT**   ambient *Umgebungs-*
> resistance *Widerstand*
> superconductor
> *Supraleiter* in the vicinity *in der Nähe*

4 **One of the participants at the meeting attends a conference on the future of energy supply. There is a workshop on the fuel cell. Not all conference participants work on the technical side, so an information sheet has been provided. Read this sheet and complete the flow chart below.**

The Fuel Cell

The fuel cell is actually quite an old technology having been invented by the British scientist William Grove in 1843. In this apparatus, electrical power is produced in a simple yet intriguing way. As can be seen from the diagram, there are two electrodes, the anode and the cathode, and in the middle of both there is a membrane ion conductor or electrolyte. Hydrogen gas is fed continuously over the anode while oxygen from the air passes over the cathode. The electrolyte is a partition which ensures that the two gases do not come into direct contact with each other. Through the chemical process in the fuel cell, hydrogen splits into hydrogen ions and electrons. The

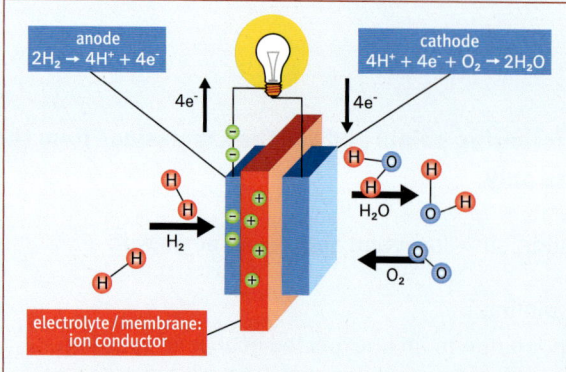

The elements of the fuel cell

electrons then pass through an external circuit to the cathode depicted by this glowing bulb. Electrical current is produced in this way.

The hydrogen ions meanwhile pass through the membrane. They and the electrons then react with oxygen at the cathode to produce water or steam. Thus heat is also produced, and this too can be utilized.

The electricity produced is direct current, which can be converted into alternating current if required. In order to create large volumes of power, fuel cells are connected in series to form a stack.

The beauty of the fuel cell is that the only waste product is water, although it should be stressed that the waste depends on how hydrogen is obtained to begin with. If it is derived from sources such as natural gas, CO_2 will also be produced.

Fuel cells can primarily be used in remote areas where there is no connection to the grid. But developments in this technology could mean that heat and electrical power from fuel cells will also be harnessed in the future in cities, in decentralized energy-supply systems for homes, offices and factories. We could even have them in our cellars.

So is this the key to a vision of clean, cheap, plentiful energy supply? Does it spell the end for the power plant as we know it? This is unlikely as the volumes of power needed cannot be generated by the fuel cell alone. But there will be changes, and in twenty to thirty years' time fuel cells could be common in energy supply as well as in vehicles.

1   An uninterrupted stream of _____ passes
over the anode while the _____ comes into
contact with oxygen from the air.

2   Hydrogen is divided into _____ and _____
as a result of the chemical process.

3   An _____ then conducts the
electrons to the cathode.

4   _____ pass through the membrane.

5   There is a _____ between the hydrogen
ions, electrons and oxygen at the cathode and
_____ or _____ is produced.

6   The type of electricity produced is DC (direct current), which
can be turned into _____ .

5   **How would you answer these questions in a discussion forum? Use information from the text and flow chart above, and phrases from Unit 4 page 32.**

I still don't really understand how it works. Can you explain in simple language?

So what exactly are the advantages, and are there any disadvantages?

Is this the answer to all our needs? Can you produce large volumes of energy like this?

Summarize the fuel cell's advantages and disadvantages in a table.

Advantages	Disadvantages
waste mostly water or steam	*depending on …*

13

6 **Delegates at the conference break for lunch. Complete this conversation using words and phrases from the box. Then listen to the dialogue and compare your version with the one on the CD.**

> actually • anyway • aren't they •
> by the way • getting on • really • sure •
> things • think of • to be honest

John   Hello Steve. Good to see you again.

Steve   Hi John. How are

_____¹?

John   Just fine. So, what did you _____

_____² the talk on the fuel cell?

Steve   All right, but _____³ the

speaker didn't really tell me anything new, although it was interesting.

John   _____⁴? I thought it was quite informative. _____⁵, how

are you _____⁶ with your paper on hydrogen?

Steve   _____⁷, I'm having a few problems. It's not easy to get all the necessary

information. Some people aren't very cooperative.

John   _____⁸? That must be quite frustrating.

Steve   Yes it is – but _____⁹. When I come to think about it, maybe you could help

me with it. I mean you have some good contacts.

John   _____¹⁰. How can I help?

DID YOU KNOW?

In many cultures small talk or conversation is seen as essential in business for creating good rapport between people. It is used to build relationships, further networking, and establish a personal setting before a meeting takes place. Topics can be smaller business issues, sports, weather, etc. But subjects which are too personal should be avoided.

---

7 **Work with a partner to do this role-play.**

You are at a conference and, during the break, you meet a business colleague whom you haven't seen for some time. Find out from your counterpart what he or she has been doing recently (work, holidays, etc). Use small-talk expressions like those in exercise 6.

PARTNER FILES   Partner A   File 6, p. 56
Partner B   File 12, p. 57

14

8 **The conference programme contains a talk on "the hydrogen-based economy". Look at these sentences. Do you think they are true or false?**

		True	False
1	Production of hydrogen is comparatively cheap.	☐	☐
2	Greenhouse gases are avoided when hydrogen is produced via electrolysis.	☐	☐
3	The use of photovoltaic cells has no real advantage.	☐	☐
4	Storage of large quantities of the gas presents a major problem.	☐	☐
5	Hydrogen research projects are being well-funded by oil companies.	☐	☐

Now listen to the talk and check your answers.

> **DID YOU KNOW?**
>
> Hydrogen is the most abundant element in the universe accounting for 75% of the mass of stars and galaxies. On earth, it is found in many substances such as water or hydrocarbons, from which it can be isolated.

9 **Your boss is expecting a report on the conference, and in particular the talk on the hydrogen economy. Write your report using the headings shown and phrases from the box.**
Note that you should also include your recommendations about future research at your company regarding this technology.

1 Introduction
2 Pros
3 Cons
4 Conclusions and recommendations

> **WRITING REPORTS**
>
> **Introduction**
> The aim of this report is to ...
> This report aims to ...
> The objective of this report is to ...
>
> **Reporting**
> It was pointed out that ...
> It was stated that ...
> It was established that ...
>
> **Linking words**
> Moreover, ...
> Furthermore, ...
> However, ...
>
> **Conclusions**
> It was concluded that ...
> It was agreed that ...
> It was decided that ...
>
> **Recommendations**
> It is suggested that ...
> It is recommended that ...
> It is advised that ...

10   **The conference is over, and the delegates are leaving. With a partner make up a dialogue in a conversational style using these prompts. Then listen to the CD and compare versions.**

1   John indicates that the conference was interesting.

_____

2   Steve agrees.

_____

3   John suggests a drink at the bar.

_____

4   Steve declines – he has to catch a plane.

_____

5   John indicates disappointment; asks about Steve's arrival time at home.

_____

6   Steve gives the time; indicates he must leave now.

_____

7   John says goodbye; asks Steve to give regards to his colleague, Sonia.

_____

8   Steve responds and says goodbye.

_____

11   **Find out what research and development projects your company or a company you work with is doing. Get information from its website, annual report or other material. Present and discuss the main ones.**

12   **Complete this puzzle. What is the word in column a?**

1   "Hi! How are ...?" – "Great, thanks."
2   The hydrogen economy within 20 ...? I don't believe it.
3   How ... does the water-pipe system have to be in the ground?
4   a cable which can conduct electricity with little energy loss
5   A place which is far away, perhaps in the middle of nowhere, is ...
6   the type of energy that you get from under the ground
7   an apparatus invented by William Grove which produces electricity
8   an idea or picture of the future

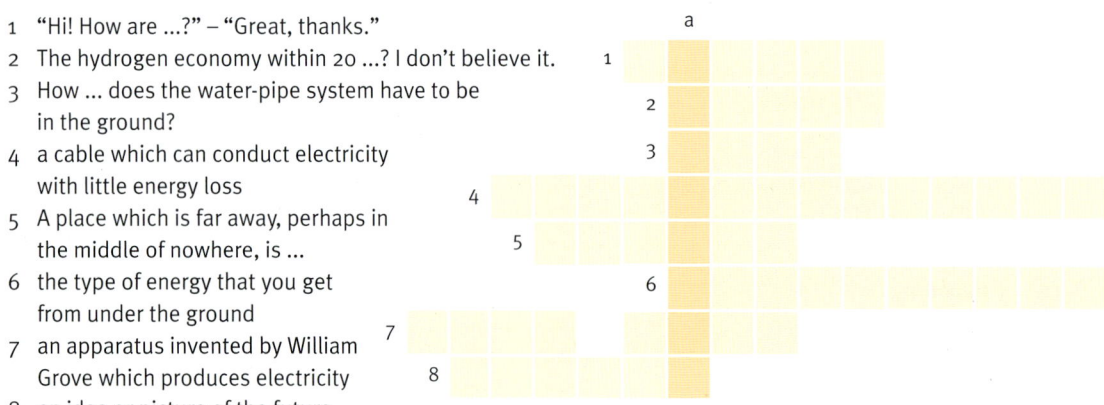

Switch off

Do you know if there are international projects concerning energy? Read this newspaper article and discuss the questions.

Lack of Vision

We are all aware of the crisis concerning energy. Climate change, constantly increasing demand, depleting reserves of

primary fuels – the issues have become so familiar that we've become bored with the whole question. We're no longer prepared to listen. But the problem is not going to go away.

There seems to be a mass of short-term solutions to this long-term problem. But it's not just a question of getting on a bus and leaving the car at home, switching off lights and DVD recorders, or doing without a winter holiday. If we take a sober look at what's going on, there is a sense of something lacking. Where is the vision? This is not just a question to be put to energy companies and politicians, but to everyone. When are we going to get to grips with solving this most urgent of problems? What is needed is a change in people's long-term thinking.

Around fifty years ago John F. Kennedy announced that the USA would be able to put a man on the moon by the end of the decade. Similarly there is now international willingness to cancel third-world debt. Why can we not create the same worldwide momentum to find new energy solutions? The hydrogen economy, fuel cells, even nuclear fusion: these are technologies which we can develop now for ourselves and for future generations.

Let's not leave the decision to the whims of the market. It is time to act now. With political will, vision, and by making a concerted effort, we can make a difference, and safeguard the livelihoods of future generations.

Over to you

- Do you agree there is a lack of vision in the energy industry? If so, what vision could be created?
- Is there a need to have international cooperation on the issue of the hydrogen-based economy? Give your reasons.

Test yourself!

See how much energy vocabulary you have learned.
Use the clues to complete the crossword puzzle.

Across

2 another word for repository, eg for nuclear waste
4 a gas like CO_2 which causes climate change
7 the development of a price or consumption
8 You'd probably find this in your cellar; it measures energy consumption.
10 the opposite of stable
11 Some energy companies plan to ... out nuclear power and then stop production.
13 to release harmful substances into water or the atmosphere
14 money used to finance future business risks, eg company pensions or dismantling power stations
15 This is the 'marriage' of two or more companies.
16 the opposite of weakness
19 another word for benchmark
22 When you have an unpaid bill or owe money to somebody, this is a ...
23 You'll find these in the balance sheet – buildings, plants, cash, etc.
26 This word describes when something is good for you.
27 a supplier of gas and electricity to customers
28 the net of lines or pipelines
29 This kind of plant produces both heat and electricity.
30 everything around you, particularly the countryside, water, forests, air, etc

Down

1 to put a power plant into operation
3 This is the decrease in value over time of an object (eg network, building, etc); the word is used in accounting.
5 to modernize a power station by equipping it with new parts
6 This is what you do to uranium so that it can be used to generate electricity.
9 This is where nuclear reactions occur.
12 a kind of brown coal
17 in the middle of nowhere
18 a gas which could replace fossil fuels in the future
20 An energy company must have this attribute to be able to supply gas and electricity all the time.
21 a kind of barrier in cables and lines which is not good for the flow of electricity
24 This is what you do to nuclear waste before it is stored long term.
25 not voluntary, compulsory

Partner files

UNIT 1, EXERCISE 4 — FILE 01

You work for ELEC in Germany. Phone your colleague in Britain and obtain the missing information. Help him/her with information that he/she needs.

Name of plant	Type	Load	Commissioned	Capacity	Location
Haymarket	_____	_____	_____	_____	45 km east of Birmingham, England
Glengarry	_____	_____	_____	_____	____ km south of Inverness, Scotland
Steinburg	lignite	base and intermediate loads	1965, retrofitted in 1984	3 units: Units A and B each producing 152 MW p.a.*; Unit C 284 MW p.a.	80 km north of Berlin, Germany
Brenes	natural gas	intermediate and peak load	(You don't know.)	2 units each producing 410 MW p.a.	24 km east of Seville, Spain

*p.a. = *per annum* = per year

UNIT 2, EXERCISE 12 — FILE 02

You are Paul. During your conversation with Anna you should discuss the agenda and make the following points. You should make some notes about what Anna says.

- Summarize the problem, and point out that a third plant in Venlo in the Netherlands is now no longer being supplied due to the collapse of the grid.
- ELEC's progress in repairing equipment: Find out the present status.
- Make AECP's position quite clear: If the problem is not remedied soon, members will be forced to look for a new supplier. Talks about this are due to start next week.
- Loss of production: You want compensation for this.
- Future contracts: You want a cheaper price and Anna and her team should prepare some proposals for the meeting.

UNIT 3, EXERCISE 8 — FILE 03

You should direct the meeting with your two colleagues. You would like to make the following proposals. Discuss these and the suggestions made by your colleagues, and decide with them on the best five.

- ELEC should focus more on renewables by building more wind generators and solar plants. They could be more economic in the long term.
- A series of seminars should be organized for ELEC staff so that they become familiar with the issues involved. They could thus become spokespersons for the company in the world outside.
- The company should start an image campaign in the media outlining positive aspects of the company.

UNIT 4, EXERCISE 12 — FILE 04

You are going to chair this meeting. The two sides come from an environmentalist group and the energy industry. Your position during the discussion should be neutral although you are free to ask questions.

- Before the discussion begins the parties will need time to prepare their arguments. During this time you could prepare a short agenda.
- After this welcome the participants to the meeting and ask them to present their points. Each should be given some time to present his/her arguments.
- Then allow time for an open discussion.
- At the end, summarize the main points and give your judgement on who was more convincing.

UNIT 5, EXERCISE 8 — FILE 05

You are Anna and should chair the meeting.

- First remind the other participants that Strathclyde Energy's IT and procurement departments are to be integrated into ELEC's Shared Services Division. Stress the urgency of the project and the need to move fast.
- Ask Richard (Partner B) to outline the key issues.
- Ask James (Partner C) for his views.
- Encourage discussion, make sure the three of you reach an agreement at the end.
- Summarize the agreement.

UNIT 6, EXERCISE 7 — FILE 06

Make some notes in bullet-point format about what you have done recently. This could be from your job, a special project, maybe a recent holiday, etc. You should give this information to your partner in a small-talk setting. Find out what he/she has been doing recently. Use expressions like those in exercise 6. Remember that your objective is to make conversation.

UNIT 1, EXERCISE 4   FILE 07

You work for ELEC in the United Kingdom. Your colleague phones from Germany. Answer his/her questions, and then ask for the information that you are missing.

Name of plant	Type	Load	Commissioned	Capacity	Location
Steinburg	_____	_____	_____	_____	80 km north of Berlin, Germany
Brenes	_____	_____	_____	_____	_____
Haymarket	nuclear	base load	1982	2 units each producing 2,300 MW p.a.*	45 km east of Birmingham, England
Glengarry	hydro	peak load	1975	2 units each producing 52,000 kw p.a.	20 km south of Inverness, Scotland

*p.a. = *per annum* = per year

UNIT 2, EXERCISE 12   FILE 08

You are Anna. During your conversation with Paul you should discuss the proposed agenda and make the following points. You should make some notes about what Paul says.

- Summarize the problem as you see it and point out that other power firms are suffering from the same problems, not just ELEC.
- ELEC's progress in repairing equipment: Reaffirm that you're doing your utmost to normalize supply, but this will take at least another four weeks.
- If AECP claims compensation for loss of production, inform Paul that an emergency fund has been set up for this purpose, primarily for residential customers. You can't say more at this stage.
- Future contracts: Point out that prices cannot change as they are very competitive and the present situation is due to force majeure.

UNIT 3, EXERCISE 8   FILE 09

You are an ELEC manager. You would like to make the following proposals at the meeting with your colleagues. Discuss these and the other suggestions made and decide with the others on the best five.

- The company should organize open days in power plants for the public.
- ELEC should join forces with its main competitors to create a common strategy on how to enhance the industry's image, particularly on environmental issues.
- ELEC should sponsor "green" events, for example gardening shows, and initiate local projects in the community to clean up rivers, establish nature trails in woods, etc.

UNIT 4, EXERCISE 12   FILE 10

You represent an environmentalist group and are going to take part in this meeting. You will now have to prepare your arguments to convince the chairperson (Partner A) that nuclear power should be phased out. Your arguments should cover aspects such as radioactivity, storage, security, etc. Your counterpart (Partner C) comes from the energy industry. Be prepared for a heated discussion.

UNIT 5, EXERCISE 8   FILE 11

You are Richard. Anna will ask you to outline the main issues. These are as follows.

- Staff will be transferred from Glasgow to Nijmegen in the Netherlands where the Shared Services Division is based.
- There will be job losses.
- Pay levels at ELEC and Strathclyde differ.
- Employees from ELEC and Strathclyde have different pension rights.

Be prepared to discuss the issues raised by James (Partner C). You have to reach a consensus.

UNIT 6, EXERCISE 7   FILE 12

Make some notes in bullet-point format about what you have done recently. This could be from your job, a special project, maybe a recent holiday, etc. You should give this information to your partner in a small-talk setting. Find out what he/she has been doing recently. Use expressions like those in exercise 6. Remember that your objective is to make conversation.

Partner files

UNIT 3, EXERCISE 8   FILE 13

You are an ELEC manager. You would like to make the following proposals at the meeting with your colleagues. Discuss these and the other suggestions made, and decide with the others on the best five. You think the last suggestion below is the best.

- The company should offer a green tariff to customers. They could buy electricity generated only from renewable sources. It would be more expensive, however.
- The company should pay customers €10.00 towards the purchase of any electrical equipment which saves power.
- ELEC could just keep quiet and not attract attention to itself. That way the company could keep a low profile and keep out of harm's way.

UNIT 4, EXERCISE 12   FILE 14

You represent the energy industry and are going to take part in this meeting. You will now have to prepare your arguments to convince the chairperson (Partner A) that nuclear power should be maintained and developed. These arguments should cover aspects of emission control, safe storage, etc. Your counterpart (Partner B) comes from an environmentalist group. Be prepared for a heated discussion.

UNIT 5, EXERCISE 8   FILE 15

You are James Sinclair from Strathclyde Energy in Scotland. In the discussion make sure that the following points are adequately taken into account.

- You have to have a workable proposal when you announce the plan to the staff representatives in Scotland.
- Employees are nervous because they don't know what is going to happen. They fear job losses.
- Having this meeting in Berlin has raised anxiety levels. Maybe it wasn't such a good idea.
- Discuss the issues and reach a consensus. Make sure you agree on a signal that will help restore staff confidence.

Answer key

page 5

Switch On

fossil fuels	renewables	nuclear fuel
(hard) coal	wind	uranium
oil	sun	
gas	biomass	
lignite	(wood)	
	(waves)	

1 1 c 2 h 3 e 4 f 5 i 6 d 7 a
   8 g 9 b

page 6

2 1 lignite
   2 gas
   3 base
   4 intermediate/medium
   5 district heating systems
   6 state-of-the-art
   7 1979
   8 retrofitted
   9 planning permission
   10 spoil

3 1 h 2 e 3 f 4 d 5 b 6 g 7 c 8 a

page 7

   9 electricity production
   10 fossil fuels
   11 base load
   12 state-of-the-art equipment
   13 energy mix
   14 company policy
   15 power station
   16 district heating

page 8

5 1 d 2 b 3 c 4 a

page 9

7 a 5 connection
   b 1 transmission network
   c 4 facility, distribution network
   d 3 municipal utility
   e 2 overhead lines, supplier

page 10

8 2 (is) fed
   3 is transported
   4 is owned
   5 are organized
   6 is delivered
   7 be chosen
   8 have been / are liberalized
   9 are also controlled
   10 are increased
   11 is also monitored

page 11

9 1 transmission   4 to monitor
      tower   5 to ensure
   2 subsidiary   6 network
   3 state   7 to charge

10 1 to generate
   2 to transmit, transmission operator
   3 to sell, seller
   4 distribution, distributor
   5 regulation, regulator
   6 liberalization
   7 to supply, supplier

   8 liberalization
   9 generation
   10 transmission
   11 regulation
   12 supply
   13 sales

page 12

11 1 ELEC Holding
   2 ELEC Power
   3 ELEC Trading
   4 ELEC Shared Services
   5 ELEC Transmission and Distribution
   6 ELEC Trading
   7 ELEC Power
   8 all the divisions
   9 ELEC Power
   10 ELEC Regional Supply
   11 ELEC Transmission and Distribution

12 1 coal   5 grid operator
   2 distributor   6 transmission
   3 base   7 generator
   4 utility   8 trading

   a customer

page 15

2 1 True.   4 True.
   2 False.   5 False.
   3 True.

Suggested answer
1. Members of AECP
   Medium-sized chemical producers with 50
   production locations in Europe, mostly in Germany,
   the Czech Republic and Benelux countries.
2. Development of wholesale prices
   AECP is concerned that kilowatt hour prices have
   been volatile over the last two years. Over the last
   five years average procurement costs have doubled.
3. AECP's objectives
   The chief objective is to reduce energy costs by
   reaching an agreement with one supplier who will

supply all the members. Security of supply is the other chief objective.

4. Forecasts on AECP's future energy consumption
   AECP expects energy consumption to increase particularly when other companies join the organization.

5. Next step
   We analyse AECP's consumption patterns over the last five years and make accurate forecasts.

page 16

3 Graph 1   kilowatt hour price over the past two years
     Graph 2   wholesale price over last two months
     Graph 3   AECP's average procurement costs over the last five years
     Graph 4   AECP's expected energy consumption over the next five years

4 1 c   Graph 4   3 d   Graph 3
   2 a   Graph 2   4 b   Graph 1

5 1   peak and then fall back
   2   hit a low and then recover
   3   increase steeply; *rocket, soar*
   4   level off
   5   fall sharply; *decrease dramatically, plummet, plunge*
   6   fluctuate
   7   fall back and then pick up again; *recover*
   8   remain stable; *hold steady*
   9   rise steadily; *grow*
  10   decline; *dip*

page 17

6 Suggested answer
The price started at the beginning of the year at €30 per megawatt hour, but rose steadily to over €40 by March. It then fell back until the beginning of May, when it increased again, levelling off at under €50 during June. In July it fell back, but rose again in August, levelling off once again in September. In October it increased steeply, peaking at €70, but fell back again through November and into December.

7 Suggested answers
1. There was a surge in the gas price because of the harsh winter.
2. The economy picked up due to an increase in high-street spending.
3. A reduction in turnover led to the cost-cutting programme.
4. There was a power cut as a result of the collapse of the grid.
5. Consumers can now choose their supplier as a result of liberalization.
6. The volatile political situation has led to uncertainty in the market.
7. More wind farms have been built as a result of financial support from the state.

page 18

8 1, 3, 6, 7
Suggested answer
AECP crisis in Netherlands
Bad weather has disrupted supply to two AECP plants in the Netherlands. They are completely cut off, and operating on back-up emergency generators

at present. Our technical staff are working to resolve the situation, but AECP has brought up the issue of security of supply and is talking about changing supplier – even though it's clearly a question of force majeure.

9 1 c   2 e   3 d   4 b   5 a

page 19

10 1   Dear Anna
   2   May I remind you
   3   Before writing this letter
   4   I might add
   5   He assured me
   6   We are extremely concerned
   7   I therefore suggest
   8   I look forward to hearing from you
   9   Yours sincerely

page 20

11 Suggested answer
Dear Paul
Thank you for your letter dated 10 April 20.. . It is indeed most unfortunate that this situation has arisen. I fully understand your concern, but I would like to stress that this is a case of force majeure as the weather conditions are not typical for this time of year. These are circumstances beyond our control. Nevertheless, we are taking this matter very seriously, and I would like to assure you that our engineers are making every effort to repair the grid and other equipment as fast as possible, so that we can again supply our customers with power.
I agree that it is important to discuss the situation face to face, and I look forward to meeting you at your headquarters in Rotterdam on Tuesday, April 17th 20.. at 10.00 am.

I'm sure our meeting will be more than satisfactory.

With kind regards,
Anna Schmidt

UNIT 3

page 23

1 1   It is with great pleasure
   2   please see attachment
   3   by invitation only
   4   to get to know
   5   Could you please let me know
   6   I would also be grateful
   7   It would be beneficial
   8   Kind regards

Suggested answer
Dear Sonia,
Thank you very much for your kind invitation to take part in the Induction Forum for Directors. I would very much like to attend.
I would be grateful if you could send me the attachment about this seminar again as unfortunately it did not reach me.
During the open forum on the Thursday evening, I would like to raise the issue of morale and would appreciate it if you could include this on the agenda. I look forward to hearing from you.

Kind regards,
Anna Schmidt

page 24

2 1 False. The public sees the company as one of the main culprits with regard to all the major environmental problems.
  2 False. Gas is the second most important source standing at 25%.
  3 False. It accounts for 20%.
  4 True.
  5 False. It is not well known.
  6 True.

page 25

3 1 greenhouse gases
  2 acid rain
  3 hole in the ozone layer
  4 carbon dioxide
  5 climate change
  6 emissions trading
  7 air pollution
  8 sea level(s)
  9 desulphurization plant

page 26

4 e – b – a – c – d

CEO Jane Hall's key point was the need to lobby governments at both a national and European level on the issues of emissions trading and subsidies, so that all companies can do business on the same basis.

5 I'm going to be covering…
Let's start with …
Let me move on to …
I'd like you to look at this pie chart.
First of all …
That completes my overview.
Please don't hesitate to interrupt me if you have any questions.

page 28

10 1 carbon dioxide – emissions
  2 sulphur dioxide – emissions
  3 combined heat and power – generation, plant
  4 volts, voltage – generation, transmission, distribution
  5 Union for the Co-ordination of Transmission of Electricity – transmission
  6 transmission systems operator – transmission
  7 distribution systems operator – distribution
  8 megawatt – generation
  9 kilowatt hour – consumption

11 1 capture   5 graph
  2 greenhouse   6 carbon
  3 subsidy   7 acid
  4 renewables   8 change

  a research

UNIT 4

page 30

Switch On
Suggested answers
waste, health, safety, radiation, disposal, security, uranium, CO_2-free

1 1 c   2 a   3 a   4 c   5 b   6 b (Calder Hall in the northwest of England)

page 31

2 1 b   2 a   3 h   4 d   5 c   6 f   7 g   8 e

page 32

3 1 control elements   4 transformers
  2 steam generator   5 cooling towers
  3 generator   6 condenser

page 33

5 a Firstly / First of all – d Then / After that – c the next step/stage is – b Finally

6 Suggested answers
Storage and reprocessing:
Present storage arrangements are only a short-term solution.
The waste has to be transported long distances.

Long-term disposal
The site has to be away from any natural threats.
Public resistance: people don't want a long-term facility in their backyard.
People worry about security.

page 34

7 1 f   2 h   3 e   4 d   5 a   6 c   7 b   8 g

  9 waste disposal
  10 interim storage
  11 Spent fuel
  12 reprocessing plants
  13 disposal facility
  14 public resistance
  15 safety measures
  16 government legislation

page 35

8 Suggested answers.
The problem is that each country has its own policy on nuclear energy, the proposed solution is to set up a coordinated lobbying strategy.

Dear Jane,
You asked me to give you my thoughts on the consultants' proposals. First of all, I'd like to stress that I don't think that the EU will ever have a uniform policy as some member states will never transfer jurisdiction to Brussels on this issue; it's just too controversial. However, as we are heavily involved in the nuclear industry, it is in our interests to support any moves to develop a coordinated strategy.
As the consultants point out, closure of nuclear plants and the knock-on effect on capability would have a dramatic effect on both jobs and expertise. On the other hand, some countries have reversed their decisions to phase out nuclear power, for example Finland and Sweden, which is to our, and the overall industry's advantage in the long run as other countries may follow this trend.
I propose setting up a meeting with like-minded utilities in which lobbyists can discuss and pursue a uniform strategy.

With kind regards,

9 a 1   b 6   c 7   d 2   e 5   f 8   g 3   h 10
i 9   j 4   k 11

page 36

11 Suggested answers

2 Know-how could be developed on the basis of other generation technologies.

3 As technological standards improve in generation from renewables this should not be a problem.

4 Most fossil fuels are imported from countries such as Russia and Kuwait. They are not politically unstable.

5 Maybe this is correct, but the effects of nuclear waste and fallout are far worse.

6 The quantities of future nuclear waste are the problem not what has been already produced.

7 So can other sources such as wave power. All we need is the investment in such technologies.

8 Maybe the kWh price would increase, but this would not necessarily lead to a recession. It would force industrial customers to be more efficient.

9 It would become more volatile if more nuclear plants were built around the world.

10 Energy companies have been forced to set up such contingencies. There is enough money saved.

page 37

13 1 interim
2 extract
3 disposal
4 uranium
5 phase out

6 reactor
7 adhere to
8 spent
9 dismantle

a reprocess

UNIT 5

page 39

Switch On
Suggested answers
profits, synergies, number of employees, sales forecasts, assets, customer structure, competitors, equity

1 Suggested answer
Consumers: worried about another price rise if the takeover goes through. Risk that people will shift to other companies.
Staff: deeply concerned about redundancies particularly at the firm's headquarters in Glasgow. Employees afraid functions will head south to our head office in Birmingham.
Trade and Industry Minister, Hilary Alexander: thinks the move may infringe European competition laws. Plans to consult Brussels to check that our bid conforms to European directives. Opposition to large firms from abroad buying up British utilities while there are obstacles for British companies to do the same in other European countries.
Financial analysts: surprised, see potential for synergies within new corporate structure as 'minimal'. They see us as already having difficulties trying to cement our interests in Spain. They claim shareholders are 'worried'.

page 40

2 1 shifting
2 redundancies
3 assurances
4 done by the book
5 infringe

6 on
7 synergies
8 investment
9 cementing

3 <u>Strengths</u> 1, 2, first part of 4, 9
<u>Weaknesses</u> 3, second part of 4, 8, 10
<u>Opportunities</u> 7, 11
<u>Threats</u> 5, 6, 12, 13

page 41

4 In favour: 2, 4   Against: 1, 3, 5   Neutral: 6

page 42

5 1 c   2 a   3 b

Fixed assets: buildings, long-term financial assets, power plants
Current assets: accounts receivable, cash at the bank, inventory
Equity: company capital
Liabilities: accounts payable, provisions

page 43

7 An all-day meeting next Thursday, starting at 10, with James Sinclair from Strathclyde.

1 the plan to integrate Strathclyde Energy's IT and procurement departments into ELEC's Shared Services Division

2 Staff will be transferred, and some jobs will be lost.

3 It's very urgent because there's a lot of pressure from above.

4 how to proceed with the integration and the job losses, how to harmonize pay conditions and pensions

5 to show that the decision-making process rests at ELEC's headquarters in Germany

page 44

9 Suggested answer
I found the following information on ELEC's plans. They want to develop new coal fields and construct a new coal-fired power plant in Yorkshire. With oil and gas prices on the increase, they expect the present coal glut situation will change, and that a combination of lower UK personnel costs and advances in extraction technology will make the project viable.

10 1 coal storage area
2 coal crusher
3 condenser

4 turbine
5 transformer
6 stack

UNIT 6

page 46

1 1 f, h
2 g, i,
3 e, n
4 m

5 b, d
6 c, k
7 j
8 a, l

page 47

2 Jan works in the trading department.

Suggested answer for the email

Dear Jan

I am afraid I have to agree with you that our forecasting was disappointing. This was attributable to a number of reasons. To begin with there was a sharp rise in consumption due to an unexpected economic upswing. Then one of ELEC's power plants went out of action because of technical problems. In addition we had problems with the Dutch/German interconnector, which was damaged at the beginning of the year. But over and above these external reasons there was a more general problem of poor communication between departments. In my view this must be improved if we are to make accurate forecasts.

Regards
(Name)

3 Suggested answer

1 Long-distance electricity transmission: need could decrease because of trend away from centralized energy systems and towards smaller power stations nearer consumption centres
2 R&D department project: superconductors as means of reducing resistance and energy losses in the grid. Biggest problem is cooling lines.
3 Geothermal heating: water pipes under ground in back garden to harness heat! Small-scale development, and how does the company come in?
4 Hydrogen: could be really major new development in generating electricity and fuelling transport. But are scientists' claims that hydrogen can replace fossil fuels in the foreseeable future realistic?

page 49

4 1 hydrogen gas, cathode
2 ions, electrons
3 external circuit
4 Hydrogen ions
5 reaction, water, steam
6 AC (alternating current)

5 Suggested answer

Advantages
waste mostly water or steam
can be used in remote areas and vehicles
suitable for decentralized energy supply systems
Heat can also be harnessed.
Disadvantages
depending on how hydrogen is obtained, eg from natural gas, CO_2 also produced
cannot produce large volumes of power such as can be generated by a power plant

page 50

6 1 things
2 think of
3 to be honest
4 Really?
5 By the way
6 getting on
7 Actually
8 Aren't they
9 anyway
10 Sure

page 51

8 1 False 3 False 5 False
2 True 4 True

9 Suggested answer

Report on the talk about the hydrogen economy
Introduction
The aim of this report is to sum up the main points of the talk given on the subject of the hydrogen economy at the ... conference on ... (date), and to make recommendations for future action.

Pros
It was stated that there are a number of advantages. If hydrogen is produced via the electrolysis of water with photovoltaic cells then the production of greenhouse gases can be avoided. It was also pointed out that hydrogen could be used instead of hydrocarbons in modified vehicle and aircraft engines. Moreover, the gas could be used together with fuel cells in cars, trucks, etc. In addition, fuel cells could be used in decentralized energy systems for electricity production.

Cons
It was established that the biggest drawback is the storage of gas as very large pressurized containers would be necessary both in vehicles and elsewhere. There would also be a weight problem. The speaker pointed out that in her view governments and oil companies are reluctant to invest in the hydrogen economy.

Conclusions and recommendations
It was concluded by our team that the commercial viability of hydrogen as a future energy source is at present unclear. However, it is recommended that our company should invest more into R&D in this area. The technology could offer considerable opportunities for company growth in the future.

page 52

12 1 things
2 years
3 deep
4 superconductor
5 remote
6 geothermal
7 fuel cell
8 vision

a hydrogen

TEST YOURSELF!

page 54/55

Across
2 storage
4 greenhouse
7 pattern
8 meter
10 volatile
11 phase
13 pollute
14 provisions
15 merger
16 strength
19 yardstick
22 liability
23 assets
26 beneficial
27 utility
28 grid
29 chp
30 environment

Down
1 to commission
3 depreciation
5 retrofit
6 enrich
9 reactor
12 lignite
17 remote
18 hydrogen
20 reliability
21 resistance
24 reprocess
25 mandatory

Transcripts

UNIT 1, EXERCISE 2

Maria ELEC Public Relations, Maria Berger speaking. How can I help you?

Colin Oh hello, this is Colin Maitland. If you remember we spoke a few days ago …

Maria Yes, yes of course. Hello, Colin. How are you?

Colin Fine, thanks. And you?

Maria Fine, thanks. So what can I do for you today?

Colin Well, as I explained last time, I'm writing this series of articles on European utilities and I'd like to include ELEC in my reports.

Maria Yes, as I said, I'm happy to give you all the support I can. Where would you like to start?

Colin Well, first I'd like some general information, and I was wondering if you could outline ELEC's energy mix first of all.

Maria Sure. Well, we have a number of fossil fuels which we use for electricity production – we mostly burn lignite and gas.

Colin Right.

Maria Yes, and our lignite-fired plants are used for base load while the gas-fired ones cater for the intermediate, or medium, and peak load ranges.

Colin Mm, OK I've got that.

Maria Then we have a number of gas plants which are combined heat and power plants; we use them to generate electricity and also to supply district heating systems.

Colin Sorry, I didn't quite catch that, what sort of systems?

Maria District heating systems.

Colin Ah, yes.

Maria So those are the fossil fuel plants. Then we also have some nuclear plants which are also needed for base load.

Colin I see. Now what about the issue of emissions? I mean, the burning of fossil fuels produces these harmful emissions and environmental problems that people of course are very much aware of these days. Could you outline your company policy on this?

Maria We take this issue very seriously indeed. All our plants are fitted with state-of-the-art equipment to reduce harmful effects on the environment.

Colin Can you give me some exact figures?

Maria I'm afraid I can't help you there, but why don't I take you round one of our plants? You could then see exactly what we do.

Colin Yes, that would be great. Um, you have a number of power stations in your portfolio. What's the largest one?

Maria Well, in terms of installed capacity that would be Altrath near Berlin. It has four 600-megawatt units and can produce enough electricity to meet the needs of some two million people.

Colin I read up on that. It's relatively old, isn't it?

Maria Well, it was commissioned in 1979, but it's been retrofitted since then. Most of our other plants came on line in the 1980s and 1990s.

Colin What about wind?

Maria We're building more wind power stations although they are still quite controversial. It can be difficult to get planning permission in some countries. Not everyone is in favour of them as they say they spoil the countryside and create too much noise if you live near them.

Colin And what's your view on this?

Maria We believe these claims to be exaggerated.

UNIT 1, EXERCISE 11

Maria So you got the information about our power plants all right, did you?

Colin Yes, thank you. Your two colleagues were very helpful.

Maria Good. But now you'd like to know more about the structure of the company.

Colin That's right.

Maria OK. Well, this chart shows the overall set-up, and as you can see, ELEC has an unbundled structure. There's a holding company, ELEC Holding, with five divisions which are all active on the pan-European electricity and gas markets.

Colin Does that mean the divisions are companies in their own right?

Maria Yes, that's right, they are. On the far left here we have ELEC Power, which is our mining and generation division. Because, you see, in addition to our power plants we also have a number of opencast mines.

Colin OK, I didn't realize that.

Maria Yes, they produce lignite and coal, mostly in central Europe. ELEC Power also procures gas for the purposes of electricity generation from our partners in Russia and other countries.

Colin Russia, I see.

Maria Mm. But the next division is more focussed on western Europe. That's ELEC Transmission and Distribution, which has a large number of networks in Germany, Denmark, the UK, the Benelux countries, the Czech Republic, Slovakia and Spain, yes they're the main ones.

Colin But not all.

Maria No, by no means all. We are in fact in the process of consolidating this division under one management structure.

Colin Right.

Maria Then next is ELEC Trading, which is the youngest member of the ELEC family. This division procures large volumes of gas and electricity for our regional supply company – as well as for industrial companies and other utilities.

Colin So this is basically a buying operation.

Maria Yes, ELEC Trading's objective is to purchase these commodities at the cheapest price.

Colin OK. And the next division is ELEC Regional Supply, I see.

Maria Yes, it's called 'Regional', but in fact this is a

Europe-wide operation. ELEC Regional Supply has a lot of subsidiaries each responsible for a confined geographical area. In this way we ensure customer proximity.

Colin   A sound principle.

Maria   Mm. Then finally, here on the far right, you can see the ELEC Shared Services division. This provides IT, human resources and legal services for the whole group.

UNIT 2, EXERCISE 2

4

Paul   As I said on the phone, our association AECP represents a number of medium-sized chemical producers in Europe. We've recently pooled our requirements and set up an energy procurement unit to look into ways of reducing energy costs. I'm sure you know our industry depends on large inexpensive volumes of power to remain competitive. I mean kilowatt hour prices were very volatile over the last two years.

Anna   Yes, but the wholesale price has remained stable over the last two months.

Paul   That's true, but we'd like to ensure that prices don't fluctuate again – at least for our members.

Anna   Yes, I understand. How big is your organization?

Paul   At the moment there are fifty medium-sized production locations in Europe, mostly in Germany, the Czech Republic and the Benelux countries, and we're looking for one supplier that can provide power for all of them.

Anna   Well, that shouldn't pose any problems. What's the present situation for your members? I imagine they have contracts with local suppliers.

Paul   That's right. But there's a big difference in the conditions that each one offers. And the average procurement costs have doubled over the last five years, standing at around 18 cents per kilowatt hour now.

Anna   What's your price target?

Paul   Before I mention that I'd also like to emphasize that security of supply must be of a very high standard. We just can't afford breaks in transmission. We'd also insist on good customer service with one ELEC key account manager responsible for the whole contract in Europe. That person would be our contact for all countries in which we operate. That covers our main objectives.

Anna   With one contact at AECP?

Paul   That's right.

Anna   I'm sure we could offer something that would go along those lines, but prices would depend on amounts supplied and the contract period.

Paul   Well, energy consumption is sure to grow over the next few years, particularly when our organization expands. Other medium-sized companies are waiting to join.

Anna   OK, I suggest then that ELEC looks into your overall consumption patterns over the last five years. That way we could make some accurate forecasts.

Paul   Sounds good. We should start this process as soon as possible.

UNIT 2, EXERCISE 8

5

Marten   We've got a real crisis on our hands, Anna.

Anna   Oh, what's up?

Marten   It's about that new international contract we have with the Association of European Chemical Producers. Our transmission grid's gone down in the Netherlands. It's due to the weather; the system has been affected by snow and ice and some of the transmission towers have collapsed. We've got teams out there working on repairs, but it's going to take a while.

Anna   OK, who's affected?

Marten   There are two AECP production sites affected. They're totally cut off.

Anna   OK, but surely we can compensate by feeding more power in from Germany through the interconnector for the time-being. I mean, we can use third-party access using another network.

Marten   Well, it's not as simple as that, I'm afraid.

Anna   Why not?

Marten   The Dutch-German interconnector is also out of action. This means we can't supply the plants at all at the moment.

Anna   So, how are they getting power?

Marten   They've switched on back-up generators, but it's only a temporary solution.

Anna   Mm, I see. There are bound to be questions of liability and insurance. But it's obviously a case of force majeure.

Marten   Yes, well I've been in touch with our contact at AECP, Paul Nieuwenhuis. He's very concerned about the situation to say the least and is worried about security of supply to all of the other production facilities in other countries, not only in the Netherlands. He says all AECP members see this development as very worrying and are thinking about looking for a new agreement with another supplier.

Anna   OK. I'll get in touch with him as soon as possible to reassure him. I'm sure we'll sort it out somehow.

UNIT 3, EXERCISE 4

6

Jane   Let me once more welcome you to the 10th Induction Forum for Directors. I'm going to be covering a number of issues in my talk, but please don't hesitate to interrupt me if you have any questions.
Let's start with ELEC's problem regarding environment issues. I'm the first to admit that there is room for improvement here, particularly if we consider that coal and gas account for most of our generating capacity, as is outlined in the forum brochure, which I'm sure you've all read. I'd like you to look at this pie chart which illustrates the point.

So, what about our company strategy regarding the future? As you know, our intention is to build more wind, hydro and clean coal plants. But in my view such programmes are not the main issue, and so let me move on to the more crucial questions. We need to undertake a number of measures. First of all, we need to lobby governments at a national and European level on the key issues of emissions trading and subsidies. The aim must be that all energy companies are able to do business within the same framework, and that the industry becomes more transparent as a whole. I'm convinced that we should be more proactive in influencing legislation made by Brussels and national governments. If this is done then we can develop a clearer and more cohesive future strategy and vision.

That completes my overview, and I'd now like to go into the various questions in more detail. First let's take a look at …

UNIT 3, EXERCISE 6

Man My name is Frank Rasch and I'm in ELEC's generating division. In this talk I want to give you an outline of what we're doing in the areas of emissions trading and research. I'll start by summarizing how emissions trading works. Many of you will be well aware of the processes involved, but for those managers and staff working in the non-related divisions this is how it works.

First of all, the general target is to reduce pollution, and to do this there are certain limits that we as power companies must stick to when it comes to the volume of greenhouse gases we can emit. We are allocated certain credits or allowances by governments; these allowances mean emissions must not exceed certain levels. Emissions trading is used when a power company gets into the situation that it exceeds the limits just outlined. The company must then buy credits from a company that pollutes less. If there's more demand, the price for these allowances increases of course, so it becomes a market in itself. ELEC has been at the forefront of this process for a number of years now.

If I could now turn to research, I'd like to outline some of the ways in which our company intends to reduce emissions. The first is carbon capture. Here, carbon dioxide is collected and then pumped deep underground thus preventing it from reaching the atmosphere. But we are also working with specialist engineering firms to design power plant equipment that will cut CO_2 emissions to almost zero. This technology's still at the research stage, but it's hoped to have such a plant in operation in the next five to seven years.

Now, if you have any questions at this point I'll …

UNIT 4, EXERCISE 3

Guide If you look at this screen you can see a diagram showing this pressurized water reactor and its operation. On the left-hand side you can see the reactor pressure vessel which produces heat from nuclear fission. This occurs in the reactor core where the fuel assemblies are situated – they contain the actual uranium. Above these assemblies you can see the control elements. When these are fully lowered, nuclear fission is completely interrupted, the

plant therefore operates at maximum output when they're withdrawn. All this is monitored and controlled by our expert teams in the central control rooms.

Now, it's important to realize that pressurized water reactors have two water circuits – the primary and secondary circuit, which are completely separated from each other. This prevents radiation from escaping. In the first, water transports the heat produced by nuclear fission in a closed circuit to the steam generator, where the heat is then transferred to the secondary circuit. So in the steam generator, heat from the primary circuit turns water of the secondary circuit into steam. This steam, I'd like to stress again, is totally non-radioactive due to the separation of the circuits. Any questions so far? Yes.

Questioner 1 Yes, em, how many fuel assemblies are there in the reactor?

Guide There are 193. Any more questions? No? OK, so the steam produced in the steam generator passes to and drives the turbine. This is connected to the generator which actually produces the electricity. From there the electricity is fed into the transformers, which raise voltage levels to the required 380 kV. Now, if you look below the box with the turbine and the generator, you can see the condenser. In this part of the plant cooling water is used to transform the steam of the secondary circuit back to a liquid state. In a sense the cooling water forms a third circuit, but we don't in fact call it that. Anyway, this cooling water in the condenser transforms the steam of the secondary circuit back to water, which is then pumped back to the steam generator. The cooling water on the other hand can be discharged back into the river which you saw nearby the plant, or it's fed into the cooling towers. This depends on the level of the water's temperature.

Questioner 2 Excuse me, what's the output of the plant?

Guide The net output amounts to some 1,330 MW. Now, if you'll follow me …

UNIT 4, EXERCISE 6

Fiona OK, well before we can start formulating our strategy on waste disposal, we have to identify the key issues. To start with, could you, Carlos, give us a rundown of what those are?

Carlos Sure. Well, the first issue is the initial and interim storage of the high-level radioactive waste, and then we have reprocessing. For our purposes we can take these together. What happens at the moment, after the fuel is extracted from the reactor, is that the waste is initially stored next to power plants. There are a number of sites in Europe where interim storage of the spent fuel is possible, but this is of course no long-term solution, and eventually the fuel has to be treated at a reprocessing plant, such as Sellafield or La Hague. The big problem is that the waste has to be transported over long distances to these plants if a country doesn't have its own facility. And then it has to be transported again to where it is stored long term.

Marita So if I can summarize that, we have two problems: first the fact that the way we store waste at the moment is only a short-term measure, and then the problem of transport.

Carlos Right. But of course the really major challenge is what happens to the reprocessed fuel long term. We really do require a disposal facility for final storage.

Marita What would that entail?

Carlos Well, safety measures would require the waste to be buried deep underground away from any natural threats such as earthquakes and the like. I mean, the waste would be vitrified, but that wouldn't make it any less radioactive of course, but it would be more confined and compressed so that the danger of leakages would diminish. And it would then be buried under clay.

Fiona And it's this question of final storage where there's most public resistance.

Carlos Yes, absolutely. Nobody wants anything like that in their backyard. But something will have to be done soon.

Marita Security of course is also an issue for a lot of people. I mean they hear stories of uranium being stolen, particularly in Russia, and are afraid this could happen anywhere.

Carlos Well, we of course have security teams at all our nuclear stations and storages to guard against any terrorist attack, as specified by government legislation. These security measures are very thorough and are strictly adhered to.

Fiona Yes, sure. But we know that not everybody ...

UNIT 5, EXERCISE 1

10

Journalist Strathclyde Energy was in the headlines last month for putting up its bills. Today it's back in the limelight as the multinational energy company, ELEC, makes a takeover bid for the Scottish firm. Consumers are worried about another hike in prices if the takeover goes through. Here's Gareth Macleod of the Consumers' Association.

Gareth Well, a lot of people will be shifting to other companies if a price increase occurs because of a takeover. We saw it happen in the past in other parts of the UK and so it would be no surprise if it happened here.

Journalist Staff in the company are also deeply concerned about redundancies particularly at the firm's headquarters in Glasgow. ELEC's UK head office is based in Birmingham, and employees fear that functions will head south although there have been assurances made by ELEC that staff have nothing to fear. The Trade and Industry minister, Hilary Alexander, is also making sure that everything is done by the book. She fears the move may infringe European competition laws.

Hilary Yes, I'll be consulting Brussels to seek assurances that this move is above board and conforms to European directives. It's just not on that large firms from abroad start buying up British utilities while there are obstacles for our companies to do the same in France, Germany or other European countries.

Journalist ELEC's move to take over Strathclyde has surprised analysts: some claim that the potential for synergies within a new corporate structure would be minimal and they doubt whether a takeover would be a viable investment. The company is already having difficulties cementing its interests in Spain with its operations in the rest of Europe, a fact which worries a lot of shareholders.

UNIT 5, EXERCISE 7

11

Anna Now, as you know, Richard, there have been a number of takeovers recently, and the board is pushing for consolidation throughout the group. One of the plans is to integrate Strathclyde Energy's IT and procurement departments into our Shared Services Division in Nijmegen.

Richard Right. That'll entail transferring staff away from the Glasgow offices then. Has the relevant trade union in the UK been notified yet?

Anna No, and that's where we expect some problems. You see, the move will also involve some job losses. But the point is we've got to start work on this straightaway; there's a lot of pressure from above. I've arranged a meeting here for next Thursday with the responsible manager at Strathclyde, James Sinclair, to discuss rolling out the project. It'll be all day, starting at 10.

Richard OK, so what's on your agenda?

Anna Well, firstly of course how we go about this integration and the job losses, but then there are questions about the staff that will be retained. One issue, you see, is that ELEC's pay levels are, on the whole, more generous than those at Strathclyde, and overall working conditions of the staff better. We have to decide what to do about those people that move to the Shared Services Division. Do we have to make changes? There's also the aspect of company pension rights.

Richard OK, I'm with you.

Anna That's why we need to have this meeting with James. I'm hoping he'll help us find solutions that are good for the company and acceptable to the staff. It's clear we're going to have to tread carefully; Strathclyde has a long history as an independent company. Its employees won't like these new and sudden developments particularly if they feel their job is jeopardized.

Richard Yes, I know. But why are you planning to have the meeting here? Wouldn't it offer a positive signal if we met James in Glasgow?

Anna I've thought hard about that, but it's more important to set a signal that the decision-making process rests here at our headquarters in Germany.

Richard Ah, OK.

UNIT 6, EXERCISE 3

12

Anna Yes, that's right, but there are also other very interesting new developments in that area. We've been monitoring for some time what seems to be the beginning of a local energy approach, with cities across Europe wanting to break away from centralized energy systems. There are already some concrete plans to build smaller power stations in the vicinity of consumption, which would reduce the need for long-distance electricity transmission.

Mark Transmission issues are certainly something that should be on the agenda. One development that R&D is looking at is how to reduce resistance and energy losses in the grid system through the use of superconductors. At the moment, the biggest problem is cooling the lines and cables to very low temperatures, which is expensive.

John And calls into question whether it'll ever be commercially viable.

Mark Sure. But it's something we mustn't lose sight of.

John No, no, of course. But going back for a moment to the movement towards local energy that Anna was talking about, there's also this trend towards harnessing geothermal energy by putting water pipe systems a few metres below the surface of the ground.

Mark Dig a hole in your back garden and that's the end of your energy problems!

John Well, underground ambient temperatures are pretty stable at around 8 to 10 degrees centigrade, and the idea that you can install your own system and save on heating costs is very attractive to home owners. I mean, as a consumer I'd certainly think of doing it.

Robin Yes, but where do we as a company come in? And besides, that's more a small-scale thing. What we really need to be looking at is the big scale, and I'm surprised nobody's mentioned hydrogen yet. I mean we've been talking for a long time about hydrogen replacing fossil fuels, but there are now scientists out there claiming that this really is just round the corner and that we'll be filling up our cars with hydrogen instead of gas, or petrol as you guys say, within the next ten to twenty years, I mean in addition to using it to generate electricity.

Anna Yes, I know, but I mean, isn't that ...

UNIT 6, EXERCISE 6

13

John Hello Steve. Good to see you again.

Steve Hi John. How are things?

John Just fine. So, what did you think of the talk on the fuel cell?

Steve All right, but to be honest the speaker didn't really tell me anything new, although it was interesting.

John Really? I thought it was quite informative. By the way, how are you getting on with your paper on hydrogen?

Steve Actually, I'm having a few problems. It's not easy to get all the necessary information. Some people aren't very cooperative.

John Aren't they? That must be quite frustrating.

Steve Yes it is, but anyway. Come to think of it, maybe you could help me with it. I mean you have some good contacts.

John Sure. How can I help?

UNIT 6, EXERCISE 8

14

Speaker So, welcome back. I hope you had a good lunch and are ready for an exciting new topic, because now I'd like to move on to the issue of the hydrogen economy.

As I'm sure you know, some universities are undertaking R&D into finding a substitute for fossil fuel. Hydrogen seems to be the best candidate although at present production is quite expensive. The gas can be obtained from fossil fuels such as natural gas, but in this process CO_2 is released, which is not beneficial. Research is therefore focussed on producing hydrogen from water via electrolysis because the production of greenhouse gases can be avoided in this way. The only products are oxygen and hydrogen. One of the most interesting ways of doing this is to use photovoltaic cells. The current generated from these cells could be used for the purpose of electrolysis.

If we move on now to the possible applications, hydrogen could be used in a number of ways instead of hydrocarbons. Aircraft engines could be modified to burn the fuel. Road vehicles could also burn hydrogen in internal combustion engines with certain technical changes. The big advantage, again, would be that the combustion process produces no greenhouse gases. Hydrogen could also be utilized to power vehicles with electric motors in conjunction with fuel cells. And, again in combination with fuel cells, hydrogen could be harnessed for electricity production in decentralized energy systems.

Storage of the gas, however, is one of the biggest challenges. It can be stored in pressurized containers, but the problem is that the quantities needed for practical application are very large when compared with the fuels we use today. This is particularly true for vehicles and aircraft. Weight would also pose a problem. But perhaps the biggest obstacle for this technology is the reluctance of governments and oil companies to support research. So it would seem that whether the hydrogen economy ever becomes a reality will depend on the market.

UNIT 6, EXERCISE 10

15

John Well, that was an interesting conference, wasn't it?

Steve Yes, it was.

John So, how about a drink at the bar?

Steve Well, I'm afraid I have to catch my plane. I'm pressed for time.

John That's a shame. What time do you think you'll be getting back home?

Steve Around midnight if all goes well. So, look, I've got to go. It was good to see you again.

John Likewise. Well, see you around. Oh, by the way, give my regards to Sonia.

Steve I'll do that. OK, see you.

A–Z word list

A   **abbreviation** [əˌbriːviˈeɪʃn]   Abkürzung
abundant [əˈbʌndənt]   reichlich vorhanden
abundantly [əˈbʌndəntli]   im Überfluss, reichlich (vorhanden)
to **abuse** [əˈbjuːz]   missbrauchen
access [ˈækses]   Zugang
to **account for** [əˈkaʊnt fə]   ausmachen
accurate [ˈækjərət]   genau, (zu)treffend, akkurat, richtig
acid rain [ˌæsɪd ˈreɪn]   saurer Regen
to **acquire** [əˈkwaɪə]   erwerben, akquirieren
acquistion [ˌækwɪˈzɪʃn]   Kauf, Erwerb
acronym [ˈækrənɪm]   Kurzwort
action: out of ~ [ˌaʊt əv ˈækʃn]   außer Betrieb
to **address sth** [əˈdres]   sich mit etw befassen
to **adhere** to **sth** [ədˈhɪə tə]   etw einhalten
to **adopt** [əˈdɒpt]   einführen, übernehmen
adverse [ˈædvɜːs]   ungünstig, nachteilig, negativ
to **affect** [əˈfekt]   beeinträchtigen, sich auswirken auf
agency [ˈeɪdʒənsi]   Agentur, Büro
agenda [əˈdʒendə]   Tagesordnung
agreement [əˈgriːmənt]   Übereinstimmung, Vereinbarung, Abkommen, Vertrag
aim [eɪm]   Ziel, Absicht
air [eə]   Luft
to **allocate** [ˈæləkeɪt]   zuteilen
allowance [əˈlaʊəns]   Bewilligung
along those lines [əˌlɒŋ ðəʊz ˈlaɪnz]   in diesem Sinne
to **alter** [ˈɔːltə]   ändern, verändern
alternating [ˈɔːltəneɪtɪŋ]   alternierend, Wechsel-
alternatively [ɔːlˈtɜːnətɪvli]   alternativ, als weitere Möglichkeit
aluminium [ˌæljəˈmɪniəm]   Aluminium
ambassador [æmˈbæsədə]   Botschafter/in
ambient [ˈæmbiənt]   außen, Umgebungs-
amendment [əˈmendmənt]   Änderung
amount [əˈmaʊnt]   Menge
Anglo-Saxon [ˌæŋgləʊ ˈsæksn]   angelsächsisch
annual [ˈænjuəl]   jährlich, Jahres-
anode [ˈænəʊd]   Anode
apparatus [ˌæpəˈreɪtəs]   Apparat
to **appoint** [əˈpɔɪnt]   einstellen, ernennen
to **appreciate** [əˈpriːʃieɪt]   schätzen, begrüßen, dankbar sein (für)
approach [əˈprəʊtʃ]   Ansatz
to **approach** [əˈprəʊtʃ]   sich wenden an
to **arise** [əˈraɪz]   aufkommen, sich ergeben
to **associate** [əˈsəʊʃieɪt]   verbinden
association [əˌsəʊsiˈeɪʃn]   Verband
assurance [əˈʃʊərəns]   Zusicherung
to **assure** [əˈʃʊə]   zusichern, versichern, versprechen
attachment [əˈtætʃmənt]   Anlage
attention [əˈtenʃn]   Aufmerksamkeit

attributable: to be ~ to sth [bi əˈtrɪbjətəbl tə]   etw zuzuschreiben sein, auf etwas zurückzuführen sein
auditing [ˈɔːdɪtɪŋ]   Rechnungsprüfung, Revision
automotive [ˌɔːtəˈməʊtɪv]   Auto(mobil)-
availability [əˌveɪləˈbɪləti]   Vorhandensein, Verfügbarkeit
aware: to be ~ [bi əˈweə]   sich bewusst sein
axis [ˈæksɪs]   Achse

B   **backup** [ˈbækʌp]   Reserve-, Notfall-
balance sheet [ˈbæləns ʃiːt]   Bilanz
base load [ˈbeɪs ləʊd]   Grundlast
beforehand [bɪˈfɔːhænd]   vorher, zuvor
behalf: on ~ of [ɒn bɪˈhɑːf əv]   im Namen von
benchmark [ˈbentʃmɑːk]   Maßstab
beneficial [ˌbenɪˈfɪʃl]   nützlich, vorteilhaft
benefit [ˈbenɪfɪt]   Nutzen, Vorteil
beyond one's control [bɪˌjɒnd wʌnz kənˈtrəʊl]   unvorhersehbar, außerhalb jds Kontrolle
bid [bɪd]   Angebot, Gebot
binding [ˈbaɪndɪŋ]   verbindlich, bindend
bound: to be ~ to be [bi ˈbaʊnd tə]   zu erwarten sein
to **brainstorm** [ˈbreɪnstɔːm]   (Ideen) sammeln
break [breɪk]   Unterbrechung
breakdown [ˈbreɪkdaʊn]   Zusammenbruch
bubble [ˈbʌbl]   (Sprech-)Blase
to **bundle** [ˈbʌndl]   bündeln
to **bury** [ˈberi]   vergraben
by the way [baɪ ðə ˈweɪ]   übrigens, nebenbei

C   **campaign** [kæmˈpeɪn]   Aktion, Kampagne
to **cancel** [ˈkænsl]   (Schulden:) erlassen
to **cap** [kæp]   eine Obergrenze festlegen
capture [ˈkæptʃə]   Speichern
carbon [ˈkɑːbən]   Kohlenstoff
carbon dioxide [ˌkɑːbən daɪˈɒksaɪd]   Kohlendioxid
carbon footprint [ˌkɑːbən ˈfʊtprɪnt] CO_2-Bilanz
catastrophic [ˌkætəˈstrɒfɪk]   katastrophal
to **catch** [kætʃ]   verstehen, mitbekommen
to **cater for** [ˈkeɪtə]   befriedigen
cathode [ˈkæθəʊd]   Kathode
to **cement** [sɪˈment]   festigen, stärken, zementieren
CEO [ˌsiː iː ˈəʊ]   Vorstandsvorsitzende/r, Generaldirektor/in
chairperson [ˈtʃeəpɜːsn]   Vorsitzende/r, Moderator/in
challenge [ˈtʃæləndʒ]   Herausforderung, Aufgabe
changeover [ˈtʃeɪndʒəʊvə]   Übergang, Umstellung
chart [tʃɑːt]   Diagramm
to **check** [tʃek]   überprüfen, kontrollieren
chemical [ˈkemɪkl]   chemisch

circuit breaker ['sɜːkɪt breɪkə] — Stromkreisunterbrecher, Überspannungsschalter
circumstance ['sɜːkəmstəns] — Umstand, Bedingung
to **claim** [kleɪm] — behaupten, erklären
to **clarify** ['klærəfaɪ] — klarstellen, erläutern
clay [kleɪ] — Ton
client ['klaɪənt] — Kunde/Kundin
co-ordination [kəʊˌɔːdɪ'neɪʃn] — Koordination
coal: hard ~ [hɑːd 'kəʊl] — Steinkohle
coal-fired [ˌkəʊl'faɪəd] — kohlebetrieben, Kohle-
cohesive [kəʊ'hiːsɪv] — in sich geschlossen
collapse [kə'læps] — Kollaps, Zusammenbruch
collusion [kə'luːʒn] — geheime Absprache
combustion [kəm'bʌstʃn] — Verbrennung
to **come into effect** [ˌkʌm ɪntu: ɪ'fekt] — in Kraft treten
commercial [kə'mɜːʃl] — kommerziell, gewerblich
to **commission** [kə'mɪʃn] — in Auftrag geben, in Betrieb nehmen
to **commit** [kə'mɪt] — sich verpflichten
commodity [kə'mɒdəti] — Ware, Rohstoff
comparatively [kəm'pærətɪvli] — vergleichsweise, relativ
competition [ˌkɒmpə'tɪʃn] — Wettbewerb
competitiveness [kəm'petətɪvnəs] — Wettbewerbsfähigkeit, Konkurrenzfähigkeit
competitor [kəm'petɪtə] — Konkurrent/in, Mitbewerber/in
complaint [kəm'pleɪnt] — Beschwerde, Reklamation
to **comply with** [kəm'plaɪ wɪð] — (Vorschriften) entsprechen, einhalten
compressed [kəm'prest] — komprimiert
to **comprise** [kəm'praɪz] — umfassen
concern [kən'sɜːn] — Sorge, Besorgnis, Bedenken
concerned: to be ~ [bi kən'sɜːnd] — besorgt sein
concerted [kən'sɜːtɪd] — gemeinsam, vereint
condenser [kən'densə] — Kondensator, Kühler
condition [kən'dɪʃn] — Bedingung
conditions [kən'dɪʃnz] — Arbeitsbedingungen
to **conduct** [kən'dʌkt] — leiten
conductor [kən'dʌktə] — Leiter
confined [kən'faɪnd] — begrenzt, beschränkt
connection [kə'nekʃn] — Verbindung, Anschluss
consequence ['kɒnsɪkwəns] — Folge, Konsequenz
to **conserve** [kən'sɜːv] — schonen
to **consider** [kən'sɪdə] — erwägen, in Erwägung ziehen, prüfen
to **consolidate** [kən'sɒlɪdeɪt] — zusammenlegen, zusammenschließen
construction [kən'strʌkʃn] — Bau
consultant [kən'sʌltənt] — Berater/in
to **consume** [kən'sjuːm] — verbrauchen, konsumieren
consumer [kən'sjuːmə] — Verbraucher/in, Konsument/in
consumption [kən'sʌmpʃn] — Verbrauch, Konsum
contact ['kɒntækt] — Ansprechpartner/in
to **contaminate** [kən'tæmɪneɪt] — verseuchen, verunreinigen
to **contemplate** ['kɒntəmpleɪt] — erwägen, in Betracht ziehen
contentious [kən'tenʃəs] — kontrovers, umstritten

continuously [kən'tɪnjuəsli] — laufend, ständig
contract ['kɒntrækt] — Vertrag
controversial [ˌkɒntrə'vɜːʃl] — umstritten, kontrovers
conversational [ˌkɒnvə'seɪʃənl] — Gesprächs-, Unterhaltungs-
convinced of [kən'vɪnst əv] — überzeugt von
core [kɔː] — Kern
corporate ['kɔːpərət] — Firmen-, Konzern-
to **correspond to sth** [ˌkɒrɪ'spɒnd tə] — mit etw übereinstimmen
cost-cutting ['kɒstkʌtɪŋ] — Kosten senkend, Kostensenkungs-
costing ['kɒstɪŋ] — Kostenkalkulation, Kostenberechnung
counter ['kaʊntə] — Gegen-
counterpart ['kaʊntəpɑːt] — Gegenüber, Pendant
to **cover** ['kʌvə] — decken, abdecken; behandeln
credit ['kredɪt] — Guthaben
criticism ['krɪtɪsɪzəm] — Kritik
crucial ['kruːʃl] — entscheidend
to **crush** [krʌʃ] — zerdrücken, zerquetschen
culprit ['kʌlprɪt] — Übertäter/in, Schuldige/r
cumbersome ['kʌmbəsəm] — beschwerlich
current ['kʌrənt] — Strom
current assets [ˌkʌrənt 'æsets] — Umlaufvermögen

D to **deal with** ['diːl wɪð] — umgehen mit
debt [det] — Schuld
decision-making [dɪ'sɪʒn meɪkɪŋ] — Entscheidungsfindung
to **decline** [dɪ'klaɪn] — fallen, sinken, abnehmen; ablehnen
to **decommission** [ˌdiːkə'mɪʃn] — außer Betrieb nehmen, stilllegen
to **decrease** [dɪ'kriːs] — abnehmen, zurückgehen, fallen
delighted: to be ~ [bi dɪ'laɪtɪd] — sehr erfreut sein, sich sehr freuen
demand [dɪ'mɑːnd] — Bedarf, Nachfrage
denox [dɪ'nɒks] — Entstickung
to **depend on** [dɪ'pend ɒn] — abhängig sein von, angewiesen sein auf
to **deplete** [dɪ'pliːt] — dezimieren, verbrauchen, verringern, erschöpfen
deposit [dɪ'pɒzɪt] — Lager, Lagerstätte, Vorkommen
depreciation [dɪˌpriːʃi'eɪʃn] — Abschreibung
to **derive** [dɪ'raɪv] — (Rohstoff:) gewinnen
desulphurization [diːˌsʌlfəraɪ'zeɪʃn] — Entschwefelung
diligence ['dɪlɪdʒəns] — Sorgfalt
to **diminish** [dɪ'mɪnɪʃ] — abnehmen, sich verringern
direct debit [dəˌrekt 'debɪt] — Lastschriftverfahren, Einzugsverfahren
direct current [daɪrekt 'kʌrənt] — Gleichstrom
director [də'rektə] — Direktor/in
to **discharge** [dɪs'tʃɑːdʒ] — (Flüssigkeit:) ablassen, ableiten
to **disinvest** [ˌdɪsɪn'vest] — desinvestieren, Anlagekapital zurückziehen

to **dismantle** [dɪs'mæntl] — rückbauen, demontieren
dismayed [dɪs'meɪd] — bestürzt
disposal; disposal facility [dɪ'spəʊzl] — Beseitigung, Entsorgung; Deponie
disposal: at sb's ~ [ət dɪ'spəʊzl] — zu jds Verfügung
to **dispose of sth** [dɪ'spəʊz əv] — etw entsorgen
to **disrupt** [dɪs'rʌpt] — unterbrechen, stören
to **distribute** [dɪ'strɪbjuːt] — liefern, verteilen
distribution; distribution network [ˌdɪstrɪ'bjuːʃn] — Versorgung, Verteilung; Verteilnetz
district heating ['dɪstrɪkt hiːtɪŋ] — Fernwärme
division [dɪ'vɪʒn] — Abteilung, (Betriebs-) Sparte
to **draft** [drɑːft] — entwerfen, abfassen, aufstellen
to **draw up** [ˌdrɔː 'ʌp] — abfassen, ausfertigen, aufstellen, formulieren
drawback ['drɔːbæk] — Nachteil
due: to be ~ to sth [bi 'djuː tə] — auf etw zurückzuführen sein
due diligence [dju 'dɪlɪdʒəns] — Kaufprüfung

E **early retirement** [ˌɜːli rɪ'taɪəmənt] — Vorruhestand
economist [ɪ'kɒnəmɪst] — Volkswirtschaftler/in, Wirtschaftswissenschaftler/in
economy [ɪ'kɒnəmi] — Wirtschaft
to **educate** ['edʒukeɪt] — erziehen, schulen
educational [ˌedʒu'keɪʃənl] — Bildungs-
effect: to come into ~ [ˌkʌm ɪntu ɪ'fekt] — in Kraft treten
efficiency [ɪ'fɪʃnsi] — Leistungsfähigkeit, Effizienz, Wirkungsgrad
electrolysis [ɪˌlek'trɒləsɪs] — Elektrolyse
electrolyte [ɪ'lektrəlaɪt] — Elektrolyt
emission [ɪ'mɪʃn] — Emission, Ausstoß
emissions trading [ɪ'mɪʃnz treɪdɪŋ] — Emissionshandel
to **emit** [ɪ'mɪt] — ausstoßen
emitter [i'mɪtə] — Emittent
to **encourage** [ɪn'kʌrɪdʒ] — motivieren, ermuntern
energy-saving ['enədʒi seɪvɪŋ] — energiesparend
enforcement [ɪn'fɔːsmənt] — Durchsetzung
to **enhance** [ɪn'hɑːns] — steigern, verbessern
to **enrich** [ɪn'rɪtʃ] — anreichern
to **ensure** [ɪn'ʃʊə] — sicherstellen, gewährleisten
to **entail** [ɪn'teɪl] — nach sich ziehen
entitled [ɪn'taɪtld] — mit dem Titel
entrant ['entrənt] — Teilnehmer/in
environment [ɪn'vaɪrənmənt] — Umwelt
environmentalist [ɪnˌvaɪrən'mentəlɪst] — Umweltschützer/in
to **envisage** [ɪn'vɪzɪdʒ] — ins Auge fassen
equipment [ɪ'kwɪpmənt] — Ausrüstung, Ausstattung, Geräte
equity ['ekwəti] — Eigen-, Aktienkapital
essential [ɪ'senʃl] — wesentlich, wichtig
to **establish** [ɪ'stæblɪʃ] — gründen, bilden

eventually [ɪ'ventʃuəli] — schließlich, endlich
evidence ['evɪdəns] — äußere Anzeichen, Beweis, Hinweis
exaggerated [ɪg'zædʒəreɪtɪd] — übertrieben
to **exceed** [ɪk'siːd] — übersteigen, überschreiten
exchange [ɪks'tʃeɪndʒ] — Börse
executive board [ɪg'zekjətɪv bɔːd] — Vorstand, Geschäftsleitung
to **expand** [ɪk'spænd] — wachsen, expandieren
expenditure [ɪk'spendɪtʃə] — Ausgabe(n)
expense [ɪk'spens] — Kosten
expense: at sb's ~ [ət ɪk'spens] — auf jds Kosten
expertise [ˌekspə'tiːz] — Fachkenntnis, Sachverstand
to **explore** [ɪk'splɔː] — erkunden, erforschen
expropriation [eksˌprəʊpri'eɪʃn] — Enteignung
extract ['ekstrækt] — Auszug
to **extract** [ɪk'strækt] — fördern, abbauen, gewinnen
extraction [ɪk'strækʃn] — Abbau, Gewinnung

F **fabrication** [ˌfæbrɪ'keɪʃn] — Herstellung
to **face** [feɪs] — sich gegenübersehen, konfrontiert sein mit
facility [fə'sɪləti] — Betrieb, Einrichtung
failure ['feɪljə] — Versagen
to **fall back** [ˌfɔːl 'bæk] — nachgeben, zurückgehen
fallout ['fɔːlaʊt] — radioaktiver Niederschlag
far-fetched [ˌfɑː 'fetʃt] — an den Haaren herbeigezogen, weit hergeholt
fault [fɔːlt] — Schuld
fault: to be at ~ [bi ət 'fɔːlt] — Schuld sein
to **favour** ['feɪvə] — bevorzugen
favourable ['feɪvərəbl] — günstig
fee [fiː] — Gebühr
to **feed in** [ˌfiːd 'ɪn] — einspeisen
fissile ['fɪsaɪl] — spaltbar
fission ['fɪʃn] — Spaltung
to **fit with** ['fɪt wɪð] — ausstatten mit, ausrüsten mit
fixed assets [fɪkst 'æsets] — Anlagevermögen
flawed [flɔːd] — fehlerhaft
flow [fləʊ] — Fließen, Fluss
to **fluctuate** ['flʌktʃueɪt] — schwanken
to **force** [fɔːs] — zwingen
force majeure [ˌfɔːs mæ'ʒɜː] — höhere Gewalt
forecast ['fɔːkɑːst] — Prognose, Vorhersage
forefront ['fɔːfrʌnt] — Spitze
the former ['fɔːmə] — der/die/das Erstere
fossil fuel ['fɒsl fjuːəl] — fossiler Brennstoff
framework ['freɪmwɜːk] — Rahmen
fuel ['fjuːəl] — Brennstoff, Kraftstoff
fuel cell ['fjuːəl sel] — Brennstoffzelle
furthermore [ˌfɜːðə'mɔː] — zudem, überdies
to **fuse together** [ˌfjuːz tə'geðə] — miteinander verschmelzen

G **gas-fired** [ˌgæs'faɪəd] — gasbetrieben, Gas-
to **gather** ['gæðə] — sammeln
to **gear: to be ~ed towards sth** [bi 'gɪəd təwɔːdz] — auf etw ausgerichtet sein

to **generate** ['dʒenəreɪt]	erzeugen, generieren	to **install** [ɪn'stɔːl]	installieren
generation [ˌdʒenə'reɪʃn]	(Strom-)Erzeugung	**installed capacity**	installierte Leistung
generator ['dʒenəreɪtə]	Erzeuger	[ɪnˌstɔːld kə'pæsəti]	
geothermal [ˌdʒiːəʊ'θɜːml]	Erdwärme-	**insurance** [ɪn'ʃʊərəns]	Versicherung
to **get in touch** [get ɪn 'tʌtʃ]	(sich) in Verbindung setzen	**intelligence** [ɪn'telɪdʒəns]	Informationen, Erkenntnisse
giant ['dʒaɪənt]	Riese	**intention** [ɪn'tenʃn]	Absicht, Vorhaben
glance [glɑːns]	Blick	**interconnected**	untereinander verbunden
global warming	Erderwärmung	[ˌɪntəkə'nektɪd]	
[ˌgləʊbl 'wɔːmɪŋ]		**interconnector**	Verbundnetz
glut [glʌt]	Überangebot	['ɪntəkənektə]	
to **go down** [ˌgəʊ 'daʊn]	ausfallen	**interdepartmental**	abteilungsübergreifend
grateful ['greɪtfl]	dankbar	[ˌɪntəˌdiː'pɑːt'mentl]	
green tax [griːn 'tæks]	Umweltsteuer	**interim** ['ɪntərɪm]	vorläufig, Zwischen-
greenhouse gas	Treibhausgas	**intermediate** [ˌɪntə'miːdiət]	mittlere/r/s, Mittel-
[ˌgriːnhaʊs 'gæs]		to **interrupt** [ˌɪntə'rʌpt]	unterbrechen, ins Wort
grid [grɪd]	Netz(werk)		fallen
		intervention [ˌɪntə'venʃn]	Eingriff, Eingreifen
H **(hard) coal** [hɑːd 'kəʊl]	Steinkohle	**intriguing** [ɪn'triːgɪŋ]	spannend, faszinierend
harmful ['hɑːmfl]	schädlich	**inventory** ['ɪnvəntri]	Warenbestand
to **harness** ['hɑːnɪs]	nutzbar machen	**investigation** [ɪnˌvestɪ'geɪʃn]	Untersuchung, Ermitt-
harsh [hɑːʃ]	streng, hart		lung, Nachforschung
to **head** [hed]	abwandern, sich bewegen	**investment** [ɪn'vestmənt]	Investition(en)
to **head for** ['hed fə]	zusteuern auf	**ion** ['aɪən]	Ion
headquarters [ˌhed'kwɔːtəz]	Zentrale	**IT (information technology)**	IT (Informationstechno-
heat [hiːt]	Wärme	[ˌaɪ 'tiː / ˌɪnfə'meɪʃn	logie)
helpline ['helplaɪn]	Hotline, Telefonberatung	tek'nɒlədʒi]	
to **hestitate** ['hezɪteɪt]	zögern		
high-street spending	Konsumverhalten	**J** to **jeopardize** ['dʒepədaɪz]	gefährden
[ˌhaɪstriːt 'spendɪŋ]		to **justify** ['dʒʌstɪfaɪ]	rechtfertigen
high-voltage	Hochspannungs-		
[ˌhaɪ 'vəʊltɪdʒ]		**K** **key account manager**	Hauptkundenbetreuer/in
to **highlight** ['haɪlaɪt]	deutlich machen, hervor-	[ˌkiː ə'kaʊnt mænɪdʒə]	
	heben, unterstreichen	to **kick off** [ˌkɪk 'ɒf]	(mit etw) anfangen
hike [haɪk]	Anstieg, Erhöhung		
to **hit** [hɪt]	erreichen	**L** **labour** ['leɪbə]	Arbeit, Arbeitskraft
to **hold** [həʊld]	halten, bleiben	to **lack** [læk]	fehlen
human resources	Personal(abteilung)	**latter** ['lætə]	Letztere/s/r
[ˌhjuːmən rɪ'sɔːsɪz]		to **lay off** [ˌleɪ 'ɒf]	entlassen
hydro ['haɪdrəʊ]	Wasser-	to **lead to** ['liːd tə]	führen zu
hydrocarbon	Kohlenwasserstoff	to **leak** [liːk]	austreten
[ˌhaɪdrəʊ'kɑːbən]		**legislation** [ˌledʒɪs'leɪʃn]	Gesetzgebung, Gesetze
hydrogen ['haɪdrədʒən]	Wasserstoff	**level** ['levl]	Niveau, Stufe
		to **level off** [ˌlevl 'ɒf]	sich einpendeln
I to **illuminate** [ɪ'luːmɪneɪt]	beleuchten	**liabilities** [ˌlaɪə'bɪlətiz]	Verbindlichkeiten
to **illustrate** ['ɪləstreɪt]	veranschaulichen, illustrieren	**liability** [ˌlaɪə'bɪləti]	Haftung
impact ['ɪmpækt]	Auswirkung, Effekt	**lignite** ['lɪgnaɪt]	Braunkohle
to **impair** [ɪm'peə]	behindern	**lignite-fired** [ˌlɪgnaɪt'faɪəd]	braunkohlebetrieben,
impartial [ɪm'pɑːʃl]	unparteiisch		Braunkohle-
to **implement** ['ɪmplɪmənt]	(Maßnahme:) durch- führen	**limelight** ['laɪmlaɪt]	Rampenlicht
to **imply** [ɪm'plaɪ]	andeuten, nahelegen	**limit** ['lɪmɪt]	Begrenzung
incentive [ɪn'sentɪv]	Anreiz	to **link** [lɪŋk]	verbinden, vernetzen
to **indicate** ['ɪndɪkeɪt]	zeigen, zu verstehen geben	**liquefied** ['lɪkwɪfaɪd]	verflüssigt
indication [ˌɪndɪ'keɪʃn]	Anzeichen, Hinweis	**livelihood** ['laɪvlihʊd]	Lebensunterhalt
induction [ɪn'dʌkʃn]	Einführung	**LNG** [ˌel en 'dʒiː]	Flüssiggas
inefficiency [ˌɪnɪ'fɪʃnsi]	Ineffizienz, Unwirtschaft- lichkeit	**load** [ləʊd]	Last
inevitably [ɪn'evɪtəbli]	zwangsläufig, unver- meidlich	to **lobby** ['lɒbi]	sich für jdn/etw einsetzen
to **infringe** [ɪn'frɪndʒ]	verstoßen (gegen)	**location** [ləʊ'keɪʃn]	Ort, Standort
innovation [ˌɪnə'veɪʃn]	Innovation, Neuerung	**long-distance** [ˌlɒŋ 'dɪstəns]	Langstrecken-
to **insist on** [ɪn'sɪst ɒn]	bestehen auf	**loss** [lɒs]	Verlust
		loyalty card ['lɔɪəlti kɑːd]	Kundenkarte
		M **management** ['mænɪdʒmənt]	Verwaltung, Geschäfts- führung, Management
		mandatory ['mændətəri]	rechtsverbindlich

measure ['meʒə] — Maßnahme
to **mention** ['menʃn] — erwähnen, nennen
merger ['mɜːdʒə] — Fusion, Firmen-
    zusammenschluss
meter reading — Zählerstand,
   ['miːtə riːdɪŋ] — Zählerablesung
mine [maɪn] — Bergwerk
minutes ['mɪnɪts] — Protokoll
to **mislead** [ˌmɪs'liːd] — irreführen, täuschen
missing ['mɪsɪŋ] — fehlend
mockery; to make a — Farce; etw zum Gespött
   mockery of sth — machen
   [meɪk ə 'mɒkəriː əv]
momentum [mə'mentəm] — Schwung
to **monitor** ['mɒnɪtə] — überwachen,
   kontrollieren
morale [mə'rɑːl] — Arbeitsmoral
moreover [mɔːr'əʊvə] — außerdem, zudem
municipal [mjuː'nɪsɪpl] — kommunal
municipality — Kommune
   [mjuːˌnɪsɪ'pæləti]

N to **name and shame** — anprangern, bloßstellen
   [ˌneɪm ənd 'ʃeɪm]
nationalization — Verstaatlichung
   [ˌnæʃnəlaɪ'zeɪʃn]
network ['netwɜːk] — Netz
nevertheless [ˌnevəðə'les] — trotzdem, dennoch
nightmare ['naɪtmeə] — Alptraum
nitrogen oxide — Stickoxid
   [ˌnaɪtrədʒən 'ɒksaɪd]
non-discriminatory — ungehindert
   [ˌnɒndɪ'skrɪmɪnətəri]
non-related [ˌnɒn rɪ'leɪtɪd] — mit etw nicht zusammen-
   hängend
notably ['nəʊtəbli] — insbesondere
to **notify** ['nəʊtɪfaɪ] — benachrichtigen
nuclear ['njuːkliə] — Atom-

O **objective** [əb'dʒektɪv] — Ziel, Zweck
objection [əb'dʒekʃn] — Einwand
obliged: to be ~ — verpflichtet sein
   [bi ə'blaɪdʒd]
to **observe** [əb'zɜːv] — einhalten, beachten
obstacle ['ɒbstəkl] — Hindernis
to **obtain** [əb'teɪn] — erhalten, gewinnen,
   beziehen
to **occur** [ə'kɜː] — geschehen, passieren
offending [ə'fendɪŋ] — Anstoß erregend,
   schuldig
opencast ['əʊpənkɑːst] — über Tage
to **operate** ['ɒpəreɪt] — betreiben
operation [ˌɒpə'reɪʃn] — Betrieb
operator ['ɒpəreɪtə] — Betreiber/in
opponent [ə'pəʊnənt] — Gegner/in
ore [ɔː] — Erz
out of action [ˌaʊt əv 'ækʃn] — außer Betrieb
outage ['aʊtɪdʒ] — Ausfall
to **outline** ['aʊtlaɪn] — einen Überblick geben,
   skizzieren
overall [ˌəʊvər'ɔːl] — gesamt, Gesamt-
overhead line — Freileitung
   ['əʊvəhed laɪn]
overview ['əʊvəvjuː] — Überblick
oxygen ['ɒksɪdʒən] — Sauerstoff
ozone layer ['əʊzəʊn leɪə] — Ozonschicht

P **participant** [pɑː'tɪsɪpənt] — Teilnehmer/in
particularly [pə'tɪkjələli] — insbesondere, besonders
payable; accounts payable — zahlbar, fällig; Verbind-
   ['peɪəbl] — lichkeiten
payroll ['peɪrəʊl] — Gehaltsabrechnung
to **peak** [piːk] — den Höchstwert/Höhe-
   punkt erreichen
peak load ['piːkləʊd] — Spitzenlast
pellets ['pelɪts] — Granulat
to **penetrate** ['penɪtreɪt] — eindringen in
pension ['penʃn] — Rente, Pension
perception [pə'sepʃn] — Wahrnehmung, Bild
performance [pə'fɔːməns] — Leistung(en)
period ['pɪəriəd] — Zeit(raum)
personnel [ˌpɜːsə'nel] — Personal
to **phase out** [ˌfeɪz 'aʊt] — auslaufen lassen
photovoltaic — photovoltaisch
   [ˌfəʊtəʊvɒl'teɪɪk]
to **pick up** [ˌpɪk 'ʌp] — sich erholen
pie chart ['paɪ tʃɑːt] — Tortendiagramm
player ['pleɪə] — Akteur/in
plentiful ['plentɪfl] — reichlich (vorhanden)
point of contact — Ansprechpartner
   [ˌpɔɪnt əv 'kɒntækt]
to **point out** [ˌpɔɪnt 'aʊt] — hinweisen auf, aufmerk-
   sam machen auf
pointless ['pɔɪntləs] — sinnlos
pollution [pə'luːʃn] — Verschmutzung
to **pool** [puːl] — zusammenlegen
to **pose** [pəʊz] — (Problem) aufwerfen
potential [pə'tenʃl] — Potenzial, Möglich-
   keit(en)
powder ['paʊdə] — Pulver
power ['paʊə] — Energie, Strom, Kraft
power cut ['paʊə kʌt] — Stromausfall, Strom-
   sperre
power plant ['paʊə plɑːnt] — Kraftwerk
practical ['præktɪkl] — funktionstüchtig
precisely [prɪ'saɪsli] — genau, präzise
predicament [prɪ'dɪkəmnt] — missliche Lage
pressure ['preʃə] — Druck
pressurized ['preʃəraɪzd] — Druck-
to **prevent** [prɪ'vent] — hindern
proactive [ˌprəʊ'æktɪv] — vorausschauend agierend
process ['prəʊses] — Prozess, Verfahren,
   Vorgang
to **procure** [prə'kjʊə] — beschaffen
procurement [prə'kjʊəmənt] — Beschaffung
profit ['prɒfɪt] — Profit, Gewinn
profitable ['prɒfɪtəbl] — profitabel
projection [prə'dʒekʃn] — Prognose, Schätzung
to **promote** [prə'məʊt] — fördern
prompt [prɒmpt] — Stichwort, Vorgabe
proportion [prə'pɔːʃn] — Anteil
proposal [prə'pəʊzl] — Vorschlag
to **propose** [prə'pəʊz] — vorschlagen
pros and cons — Für und Wider
   [ˌprəʊz ənd 'kɒnz]
to **protect** [prə'tekt] — schützen
protocol ['prəʊtəkɒl] — Protokoll
to **provide** [prə'vaɪd] — versorgen
provision [prə'vɪʒn] — Rückstellung, Rücklage
proximity [prɒk'sɪməti] — Nähe
public relations officer — Pressereferent/in
   [ˌpʌblɪk rɪ'leɪʃnz ɒfɪsə]

pulp [pʌlp]	Faserstoff	
pump-storage [pʌmp ˈstɔːrɪdʒ]	Speicher-	
purchase [ˈpɜːtʃəs]	Kauf	
to **purify** [ˈpjʊərɪfaɪ]	reinigen	
to **puzzle** [ˈpʌzl]	verblüffen, Rätsel aufgeben	
pylon [ˈpaɪlən]	Mast	

Q	**quantity** [ˈkwɒntəti]	Menge
	to **question** [ˈkwestʃən]	in Frage stellen
	questionable [ˈkwestʃənəbl]	fraglich

R	**radiation** [ˌreɪdiˈeɪʃn]	Strahlung
	to **raise** [reɪz]	aufwerfen, zur Sprache bringen
	range [reɪndʒ]	Bereich, Spektrum, Bandbreite, Palette
	to **rank** [ræŋk]	einstufen
	rapidly [ˈræpɪdli]	schnell, rasch
	rapport [ræˈpɔː]	gutes Verhältnis
	to **rate** [reɪt]	bewerten, einstufen
	to **ratify** [ˈrætɪfaɪ]	ratifizieren
	rating [ˈreɪtɪŋ]	Bewertung, Beurteilung
	ratio [ˈreɪʃiəʊ]	Verhältnis, Quote
	to **reassure** [ˌriːəˈʃʊə]	beruhigen
	receivable; accounts receivable [rɪˈsiːvəbl]	ausstehend, offen; Forderungen, Außenstände
	recommendation [ˌrekəmenˈdeɪʃn]	Empfehlung
	to **recover** [rɪˈkʌvə]	sich erholen
	to **rectify** [ˈrektɪfaɪ]	richtig stellen
	red tape [ˌred ˈteɪp]	Bürokratie
	redundancy [rɪˈdʌndənsi]	betriebsbedingte Kündigung
	regulator [ˈregjuleɪtə]	Aufsichtsbehörde
	relevant [ˈreləvənt]	entsprechend
	reliability [rɪˌlaɪəˈbɪləti]	Zuverlässigkeit
	reliable [rɪˈlaɪəbl]	zuverlässig
	to **remain** [rɪˈmeɪn]	bleiben
	to **remedy** [ˈremədi]	beheben
	remote [rɪˈməʊt]	entlegen
	renewable [rɪˈnjuːəbl]	erneuerbar
	renewables [rɪˈnjuːəblz]	erneuerbare Energiequellen
	repercussion [ˌriːpəˈkʌʃn]	Auswirkung, Konsequenz
	repetition [ˌrepəˈtɪʃn]	Wiederholung
	to **replace** [rɪˈpleɪs]	ersetzen
	to **reprocess** [ˌriːˈprəʊses]	wiederaufbereiten
	reputation [ˌrepjuˈteɪʃn]	Ruf
	request [rɪˈkwest]	Bitte, Wunsch, Aufforderung
	requirement [rɪˈkwaɪəmənt]	Bedarf
	research and development [rɪˌsɜːtʃ ən dɪˈveləpmənt]	Forschung und Entwicklung
	reservation [ˌrezəˈveɪʃn]	Bedenken
	reserve [rɪˈzɜːv]	Reserve, Vorkommen
	reservoir [ˈrezəvwɑː]	Stausee, Staubecken
	residential [ˌrezɪˈdenʃl]	Wohn-, Wohnungs-
	resistance [rɪˈzɪstəns]	Widerstand
	to **resolve** [rɪˈzɒlv]	lösen
	responsible: to be ~ for [bi rɪˈspɒnsəbl fə]	verantwortlich sein für
	restriction [rɪˈstrɪkʃn]	Einschränkung
	to **result in** [rɪˈzʌlt ɪn]	zur Folge haben, führen zu

retail [ˈriːteɪl]	Einzelhandel	
to **retain** [rɪˈteɪn]	(weiter)beschäftigen	
to **retrofit** [ˈretrəʊfɪt]	nachträglich einbauen, nachrüsten	
return on investment [rɪˌtɜːn ɒn ɪnˈvestmənt]	Anlageertrag, Kapitalrendite	
to **reverse** [rɪˈvɜːs]	rückgängig machen	
rod [rɒd]	Stab	
room for improvement [ˌruːm fər_ɪmˈpruːvmənt]	Verbesserungspotenzial	
rules and regulations [ˌruːlz ənd regjuˈleɪʃnz]	Vorschriften	
run-of-river [ˌrʌn əv ˈrɪvə]	Laufwasser-	
rundown [ˈrʌndaʊn]	Zusammenfassung	

S	to **safeguard** [ˈseɪfgɑːd]	schützen, sichern
	to **satisfy** [ˈsætɪsfaɪ]	befriedigen
	scale [skeɪl]	Skala
	scheme [skiːm]	Plan, Programm, Projekt
	sea level [ˈsiː levl]	Meeresspiegel
	to **seal** [siːl]	versiegeln
	to **sell off** [ˌsel ˈɒf]	verkaufen, abstoßen
	seriously [ˈsɪəriəsli]	ernst
	set-up [ˈsetʌp]	Aufbau; System, Regelung, Zustände
	severe(ly) [sɪˈvɪəli]	schwer, stark
	shareholder [ˈʃeəhəʊldə]	Aktionär/in, Anteilseigner/in
	to **shift** [ˈʃɪft]	wechseln
	to **ship** [ʃɪp]	verschiffen, mit Schiffen transportieren
	shortage [ˈʃɔːtɪdʒ]	Knappheit, Mangel
	signatory [ˈsɪgnətri]	Unterzeichnete/r
	site [saɪt]	Standort, Anlage
	slide [slaɪd]	Dia(positiv)
	to **soar** [sɔː]	in die Höhe schießen, hochschnellen
	sober [ˈsəʊbə]	nüchtern
	solar [ˈsəʊlə]	Sonnen-, Solar-
	solid [ˈsɒlɪd]	fest
	to **solve** [sɒlv]	lösen
	somewhat [ˈsʌmwɒt]	etwas, ein wenig
	source [sɔːs]	Quelle
	to **speak for** [ˈspiːk fə]	sprechen für
	specific [spəˈsɪfɪk]	bestimmte/r/s
	spending [ˈspendɪŋ]	Ausgaben
	spent [spent]	verbraucht, abgebrannt
	sponsorship [ˈspɒnsəʃɪp]	Förderung, Sponsoring
	spot price [ˈspɒt praɪs]	Barpreis, Spotpreis
	stable [ˈsteɪbl]	stabil
	stack [stæk]	Schlot, Schornstein
	stakeholder [ˈsteɪkhəʊldə]	Teilhaber/in, Beteiligte/r
	to **standardize** [ˈstændədaɪz]	normieren, standardisieren
	state of affairs [ˌsteɪt əv əˈfeəz]	Situation
	state-of-the-art [ˌsteɪt əv ði ˈɑːt]	hochmodern, auf dem letzten Stand (der Technik)
	statement [ˈsteɪtmənt]	Aussage, Feststellung, Behauptung
	steadily [ˈstedɪli]	stetig
	steam [stiːm]	Dampf
	steeply [ˈstiːpli]	steil
	to **stick to sth** [ˈstɪk tə]	an etw festhalten
	to **stifle** [ˈstaɪfl]	ersticken, unterdrücken

stock [stɒk]	Vorrat	
storage ['stɔːrɪdʒ]	Lagerung	
straightaway [ˌstreɪtə'weɪ]	sofort	
straightforward [ˌstreɪt'fɔːwəd]	einfach	
to **stress** [stres]	betonen	
to **stretch** [stretʃ]	sich erstrecken	
subsequent ['sʌbsɪkwənt]	nachfolgend, Folge-	
subsidiary [səb'sɪdiəri]	Tochter(gesellschaft)	
subsidy ['sʌbsədi]	Subvention	
substance ['sʌbstəns]	Substanz, Stoff	
substation ['sʌbsteɪʃn]	Umspannstation, Transformatorenstation	
sufficient [sə'fɪʃnt]	ausreichend	
sulphur dioxide [ˌsʌlfə daɪ'ɒksaɪd]	Schwefeldioxid	
sunlight ['sʌnlaɪt]	Sonnenlicht	
superconductor ['suːpəkəndʌktə]	Supraleiter	
supervisory [ˌsuːpə'vaɪzəri]	Aufsichts-	
supplier [sə'plaɪə]	Versorger, Anbieter	
to **supply** [sə'plaɪ]	versorgen, beliefern	
surrounding [sə'raʊndɪŋ]	umliegend	
sustainable [sə'steɪnəbl]	nachhaltig	
to **swallow up** [ˌswɒləʊ 'ʌp]	schlucken, verschlucken	
synchronous ['sɪŋkrənəs]	synchron	

T

to **tackle** ['tækl]	angehen, in Angriff nehmen
to **take apart** [ˌteɪk ə'pɑːt]	auseinander nehmen
takeover ['teɪkəʊvə]	Übernahme
tantamount: to be ~ to sth [bi 'tæntəmaʊnt tə]	einer Sache gleichkommen, auf etw hinauslaufen
target ['tɑːgɪt]	Ziel
task [tɑːsk]	Aufgabe, Arbeit
temporary ['temprəri]	vorübergehend
terms [tɜːmz]	Bedingungen, Konditionen
thermal ['θɜːml]	Wärme-
third-party; third-party access [ˌθɜːd 'pɑːti]	von Dritten, von Fremdfirmen; Durchleitung
thought-provoking ['θɔːt prəvəʊkɪŋ]	zum Nachdenken anregend, nachdenklich stimmend
threat [θret]	Bedrohung
through the backdoor [θruː ðə ˌbæk'dɔː]	durch die Hintertür
tidal ['taɪdl]	Gezeiten-
time: for the ~ being [fə ðə ˌtaɪm 'biːɪŋ]	gegenwärtig, im Augenblick
track record ['træk rekɔːd]	Erfolgsbilanz, Erfolgs- und Leistungsnachweis
trade union [ˌtreɪd 'juːniən]	Gewerkschaft

transformer [træns'fɔːmə]	Transformator
transmission [træns'mɪʃn]	Übertragung, Leitung, Transport-
to **transmit** [træns'mɪt]	übertragen
transparency [træns'pærənsi]	Overheadfolie
to **tread carefully** [ˌtred 'keəfəli]	behutsam vorgehen
treaty ['triːti]	Vertrag
to **trigger** ['trɪgə]	auslösen
turnover ['tɜːnəʊvə]	Umsatz

U

unaffected [ˌʌnə'fektɪd]	unberührt
to **unbundle** [ʌn'bʌndl]	entflechten, zerlegen
uncertainty [ʌn'sɜːtnti]	Ungewissheit
to **underestimate** [ˌʌndər'estɪmeɪt]	unterschätzen
unit ['juːnɪt]	Einheit, Abteilung
universe ['juːnɪvɜːs]	Universum
unlike [ˌʌn'laɪk]	anders als, im Gegensatz zu
unstable [ʌn'steɪbl]	instabil
to **upgrade** [ˌʌp'greɪd]	verbessern, aktualisieren
uphill [ˌʌp'hɪl]	bergauf
upsurge ['ʌpsɜːdʒ]	Zunahme
upswing ['ʌpswɪŋ]	Aufschwung
uranium [ju'reɪniəm]	Uran
urgent ['ɜːdʒənt]	dringend, eilig
utility [juː'tɪləti]	Versorgungsbetrieb
to **utilize** ['juːtəlaɪz]	nutzen
utmost ['ʌtməʊst]	äußerste/r/s

V

value ['væljuː]	Wert
vehicle ['viːəkl]	Fahrzeug
to **verify** ['verɪfaɪ]	nachprüfen, bestätigen
versatile ['vɜːsətaɪl]	vielseitig
vertical ['vɜːtɪkl]	senkrecht, vertikal
vessel ['vesl]	Behälter, Gefäß
viable ['vaɪəbl]	rentabel, lebensfähig
vicinity: in the ~ [ɪn ðə və'sɪnəti]	in der Nähe
to **view** [vjuː]	betrachten
vitrify ['vɪtrɪfaɪ]	zu Glas schmelzen
volatile ['vɒlətaɪl]	instabil, unbeständig
voltage ['vəʊltɪdʒ]	Spannung
volume ['vɒljuːm]	Umfang, Menge
voluntary ['vɒləntri]	freiwillig

W

waste [weɪst]	Müll
watchdog ['wɒtʃdɒg]	Überwachungsgremium
water pipe ['wɔːtə paɪp]	Wasserleitung
whereby [weə'baɪ]	wodurch
whim [wɪm]	Laune
wholesale ['həʊlseɪl]	Großhandels-
wind farm ['wɪnd fɑːm]	Windkraftanlage
worrying ['wʌriɪŋ]	beunruhigend

Y

yardstick ['jɑːdstɪk]	Maßstab

Glossary

balance sheet
A financial statement listing the value of assets, equity and liabilities of a company at a particular date.

base load
The minimum amount of electricity delivered and required over a specific period.

capacity
The maximum amount of electricity that can be generated from a power station or set of power stations.

collusion
Secret and improper talks between two or more companies usually to fix prices.

commodity
Any product such as gas or electricity which can be bought or sold.

condenser
An apparatus which turns steam into water.

connection
Equipment which links a building with the local electricity or gas network.

cooling tower
A large circular structure at a power plant through which water is circulated to reduce its temperature.

core business
The main field of activities or operations of a company.

current assets
Things of value of a company which it uses in its normal day-to-day operations such as cash and materials.

decentralized energy system
Equipment which produces power for a nearby house, building or small community without the need for long distance transportation of electricity.

denox plant
An apparatus at a power station which breaks down nitrogen oxides.

desulphurization plant
An apparatus at a power plant which removes sulphur oxides.

disinvestment
The withdrawal or reduction of capital investment.

distribution
The local transportation of electricity or gas from the main network to the final user.

district heating
A system for distributing heat, produced in a centralized plant, to homes and offices.

due diligence
A careful investigation of the financial and business situation of a company which may be taken over.

efficiency
A ratio between the output of a power station and the energy input usually expressed as a percentage.

emissions trading
A system of buying and selling credits or allowances regarding CO_2 quotas in order to reduce the overall amount of pollution.

energy mix
The combination and proportions of primary fuels and sources used for electricity production.

expropriation
The taking of property from a private owner by the state or government usually through compulsory purchase.

fixed asset
An object such as a building or power plant owned and utilized by a company for long-term use; it is not expected to be turned into cash.

flue gas
Exhaust gases such as sulphur oxides, nitrogen oxides and carbon dioxide which are produced in the combustion process at a power plant.

force majeure
An unavoidable event over which the parties who have signed a contract have no influence, eg bad weather conditions or a strike.

fossil fuel
Hydrocarbons such as gas, oil or coal used for producing electricity.

fuel cell
An apparatus which produces electrical current from a reaction between hydrogen and oxygen.

generation
The production of electrical power.

global warming
An increase in the average temperatures of the earth's atmosphere.

greenhouse gas
A gas such as CO_2 which causes the warming of the earth's atmosphere through its absorption of solar radiation.

grid
A network of pipelines, cables or overhead lines.

hydrogen economy
A concept for the future in which fossil fuels are replaced by hydrogen gas for energy production and industrial activities.

industrial customer
A company that buys and uses electricity or gas for manufacturing.

interim storage
A facility for holding (nuclear) waste for a limited period before it is moved to a final location.

intermediate/medium load
The amount of electricity delivered and required over a specific period between base and peak loads.

key account manager
A member of sales staff who looks after a specific group of customers.

legislation
Laws, or the act of making them.

lobbyist
A person who acts for an organization and tries to influence politicians or other national decision-makers.

municipal utility
A company owned by a city or town which transmits, distributes and delivers electricity and/or gas.

nationalization
The act of bringing a company under state ownership and control.

nuclear fission
A reaction in which nuclei of atoms split to release massive amounts of energy; uranium is the fuel used in this process.

nuclear fusion
A reaction in which nuclei of atoms fuse together to release massive amounts of energy.

peak load
The maximum amount of electricity delivered and required over a specific period.

power plant/station
A complex of buildings, machinery and equipment used for generating electricity.

profit and loss account
A financial statement of a company which shows its expenditures and income over a period; these are balanced to show a final profit or loss.

provisions
The money a company sets aside for future risk or use such as company pensions or the decommissioning of power plants.

pylon
A tall metal structure which carries an overhead line.

red tape
Another term for bureaucracy.

regulator
Organization or person who monitors and, if necessary, sanctions energy companies.

renewables
Primary energy sources such as wind, sun and water.

reprocessing plant
A facility in which nuclear waste is treated and processed.

residential/retail customer
A consumer who procures gas or electricity for home use.

retail price
The amount of money charged to the final user by energy companies for gas or electricity.

return on investment
The income that can be expected from an investment usually expressed as a percentage.

spent fuel
Uranium that has been used up.

stack
A tall chimney at a power plant.

subsidiary
A company which belongs to a parent or holding company.

subsidy
Financial support for companies in an industry given by the government or state.

supply
The provision of gas or electricity to the final customer.

synergy
Combined advantages arising from the interaction of the companies involved in a merger or takeover.

transformer
Equipment which changes voltage levels of electricity.

transmission
The transport of electricity over long distances at high voltage.

transmission tower
A tall metal structure which carries overhead lines.

turbine
Equipment with a rotor which is driven by a jet of steam.

utility
A company which transmits, distributes and delivers electricity and or gas.

waste disposal
The transporting, processing and recycling of unwanted substances.

watchdog
An organization working in the interests of customers which monitors the activities of energy companies particularly regarding price.

wholesale price
The amount of money charged to companies which buy large volumes of gas or electricity; these companies then sell these commodities to the final customer.

Useful phrases and vocabulary

EXPRESSING OPINIONS AND (DIS)AGREEMENT

Giving your opinion
I think/feel (that) ...
In my opinion ...
In my view ...

Agreeing
Quite right.
That's true.
I quite agree.

Clarifying
So you're saying ...
You mean ...
What do you mean by ...?

Disagreeing
Actually, I think ...
To be honest ...
I don't quite agree.

DISCUSSING IN A MEETING

Proposing
Couldn't we just ...?
What if we ...?
Why don't we ...?

Asking for agreement/disagreement
Do we all agree on that?
Does anybody object to this?
Who's in favour of this proposal?

Showing concern
I have some reservations/concerns about ...
Actually, I don't think that's a good idea.

Emphasizing
I'd again like to point out that ...
I know I keep going on about this, but ...

CHAIRING A MEETING

Opening the meeting
Can we now agree on the overall procedure?
First of all, I think we should establish the overall procedure.
The main objectives of the meeting are ...
Does that seem acceptable to you?

Asking somebody to start
Would you like to start, John?
John, would you like to kick off?

Keeping to the agenda
OK, could we please come back to the agenda?
I'm afraid that's not part of the discussion.

Asking for clarification
I don't quite follow. What do you mean by ...?
I don't really get what you mean.

GIVING A PRESENTATION

Opening
Let me first introduce myself.
I'm / My name is ...
In this talk I want / would like to ...
I'll begin by (+ -ing form of verb) ...
I'm going to be covering ...
Let's start with (+ noun) ...

Introducing other factors or points
If I could now turn to ...
Now, turning to ...
Let me move on to ...

Introducing graphs and diagrams
I'd like you to look at this graph / diagram / (pie) chart / transparency / slide.
This graph shows ...
You can see here that ...

Comparing factors
First of all ...
Firstly ..., Secondly ..., Thirdly ...
On the one hand ... , On the other hand ...

Questions
Please don't hesitate to interrupt me if you have any questions.
If you have any questions, I'll be pleased to answer them at the end.

Finishing
That completes my overview (of ...).
So, to summarize / sum up ...
Thank you for your attention.

DESCRIBING TRENDS

It grew / rose / increased / picked up / recovered / peaked.
It fell / declined / hit a low.
It fluctuated / was volatile.
It remained stable.
This happened/occurred because ...
We expected this change, but ...
Although there was a fall/rise ...
This was due to ...
This was because of ...

DESCRIBING A PROCESS

Firstly / First of all ...
After that ...
The next step/stage is ...
Then ...

Following that ...
Finally ...
The final step ...

TELEPHONING FOR INFORMATION

Introductions
Hello … . This is … speaking.
Hi …, it's … here.

Asking for information
I need some information about …
I'd like to have some (more) information about …
Can/Could you give me more information about …?
Can/Could you please tell me (about) …?
Who / What / When / Where / Why / How …?
What about …?

Asking for repetition
Sorry, I didn't quite catch that.
Would you mind repeating that?

Positive response
Sure.
No problem.
I'd be happy to.

Negative response
I'm afraid I can't help you there.
I'm afraid not.

REPLYING TO INVITATIONS

Accepting
I was delighted to receive your kind invitation …
Thank you very much for your kind invitation to take part in …
I would very much like to attend.

Making requests
Would/Could you please …?
I would be grateful if you could …
I would appreciate it if you could …

DEALING WITH COMPLAINTS

Reassuring
We are taking this matter very seriously.
I can / would also like to assure you that …
We are making every effort to …
We are doing our utmost / all we can to …

Not accepting responsibility
I fully understand your concern, but …
I would like to stress that …
These are circumstances beyond our control.
Nevertheless, …
That's quite impossible.

USEFUL VERBS (IN CONTEXT)

to commission	This power plant **was commissioned** last year.	in Betrieb nehmen
to comply with	Energy companies have to **comply with** all rules and regulations.	einhalten
to condense	Steam **condenses** into water at the power station.	kondensieren
to convert	DC **is converted** into AC if necessary.	umwandeln
to decommission	Some plants **were decommissioned** as they were not economic.	außer Betrieb nehmen
to deplete	Coal stocks **have been depleted** due to a rise in consumption.	verbrauchen, verringern
to disinvest	Unwanted activities **will be disinvested**.	desinvestieren
to dismantle	A nuclear plant has to **be dismantled** at the end of its life.	rückbauen, demontieren
to dispose of	Some companies **dispose of** waste by burning it.	entsorgen
to distribute	Gas **is distributed** throughout Europe from fields in the North Sea.	verteilen
to emit	Many harmful gases **are emitted** from power stations.	ausstoßen
to exceed	Emissions must not **exceed** certain levels.	überschreiten
to fluctuate	Wholesale prices **have been fluctuating** over the past year.	schwanken
to generate	Electricity **is generated** at our power stations.	erzeugen
to lay off	Many employees **were laid off** after the takeover.	entlassen
to liberalize	Customers can choose their supplier as the market **is liberalized**.	liberalisieren
to merge	Two utilities **have merged** to form a new company.	fusionieren
to monitor	Our image in the media **is being monitored** by management.	beobachten, überwachen
to operate	The TSO **operates** the transmission grid.	betreiben
to phase out	Some countries wish to **phase out** nuclear power.	auslaufen lassen
to pollute	Generators that **pollute** too much must buy credits or allowances.	verschmutzen
to procure	Our company **procures** large quantities of gas.	beschaffen
to regulate	Some countries **regulate** the energy market through price controls.	regulieren
to reprocess	Nuclear waste **is reprocessed** before final storage.	wiederaufbereiten
to retrofit	Our older plants **have been retrofitted** to bring them up to standard.	nachrüsten
to subsidize	The coal industry **is subsidized** through state support.	subventionieren
to supply	We **supply** gas to a number of different companies.	(be)liefern
to switch	Many residential customers **switched** suppliers because of high prices.	wechseln
to transmit	Electricity **is transmitted** through the grid.	leiten, übertragen

Abbreviations, acronyms and numbers

Abbreviations and acronyms

ACER	Agency for the Co-ordination of Energy Regulators
AEP	Association of Energy Producers
AC	alternating current
CCGT	combined cycle gas turbine
CCPP	combined cycle power plant
CCT	clean coal technology
CEO	chief executive officer
CFO	chief financial officer
CHP	combined heat and power
CO	carbon monoxide
CO_2	carbon dioxide
DC	direct current
dept	department
DSO	distribution systems operator
EASEE	European Association for the Streamlining of Energy Exchange
EC	European Commission
EEX	European Energy Exchange
EU	European Union
GHG	greenhouse gas
GPA	Gas Producers Association
H	hydrogen
IAEA	International Atomic Energy Authority
IAHE	International Association for Hydrogen Energy
IEA	International Energy Agency
IGCC	integrated gasification combined cycle
Inc	incorporated
IPP	independent power producer
ISO	independent systems operator, International Standards Organization
ITER	International Thermonuclear Experimental Reactor
LNG	liquefied natural gas
Ltd	limited
misc	miscellaneous
NOx	nitrogen oxides
NGO	non-governmental organization
O_2	oxygen
OECD	Organization for Economic Co-operation and Development
PLC	public limited company
p.a.	per annum
PV	photovoltaic
Q	quarterly
RAPS	remote area power supply
REEF	Renewable Energy Equity Fund
SO_2	sulphur dioxide
TSO	transmission systems operator
UCTE	Union for the Co-ordination of Transmission of Electricity
UNEP	United Nations Environment Programme
WCI	World Coal Institute
WTO	World Trade Organization

A	amperes
bbl	barrel
bn	billion (1 000 000 000)
°C	degrees Celsius (centigrade)
GW	gigawatt
Ha	hectare
Hz	hertz
J	joule
kW	kilowatt
kWh	kilowatt-hour
l	litre
m	million (1 000 000)
m	metre
m^3	cubic metres
m^2	square metres
MW	megawatt
t	ton
TCE	tons of coal equivalent
TW	terawatt
V	volt, voltage
W	watt
Ω	ohm

Numbers

356	three hundred (and) fifty-six
1,356	one thousand three hundred (and) fifty-six
1,256,349	one million two hundred (and) fifty-six thousand three hundred (and) forty-nine
1.356	one **point** three five six
1.035	one **point zero / nought** three five

mega	1 000 000	10^6	ten to the power of six
giga	1 000 000 000	10^9	ten to the power of nine
tera	1 000 000 000 000	10^{12}	ten to the power of twelve

€1,356.59	one thousand three hundred (and) fifty-six euro**s** fifty-nine
€10 m	ten million euro**s**
€10 bn	ten billion euro**s**

2001	two thousand and one
2009	two thousand and nine
2010	twenty ten
2015	twenty fifteen
2020	twenty twenty